The Power of Praying® for Your Adult Children

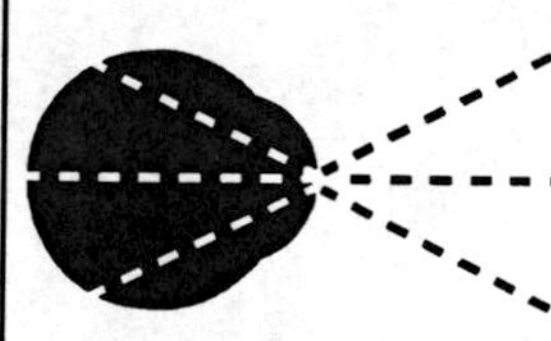

This Large Print Book carries the
Seal of Approval of N.A.V.H.

The Power of Praying® for Your Adult Children

Stormie Omartian

CHRISTIAN LARGE PRINT
A part of Gale, Cengage Learning

Detroit • New York • San Francisco • New Haven, Conn • Waterville, Maine • London

Christian Large Print, a part of Gale, Cengage Learning.

Christian Large Print Originals.
The text of this Large Print edition is unabridged.
Other aspects of the book may vary from the original edition.
Set in 16 pt. Plantin.
Printed on permanent paper.

LIBRARY OF CONGRESS CATALOGING-IN-PUBLICATION DATA

Omartian, Stormie.
The power of praying for your adult children / by Stormie Omartian. — Large print ed.
p. cm.
"Christian Large Print originals."
ISBN-13: 978-1-59415-317-4 (softcover : alk. paper)
ISBN-10: 1-59415-317-5 (softcover : alk. paper)
1. Parents—Prayers and devotions. 2. Adult children—Religious life. 3. Large type books. I. Title.
BV283.C5O54 2010
248.3'2—dc22 2009042787

Published in 2010 by arrangement with Harvest House Publishers.

Printed in the United States of America
2 3 4 5 6 18 17 16 15 14

CONTENTS

All your children shall be
taught by the L*ORD*,
and great shall be
the peace of your children.

ISAIAH 54:13

What Every Parent of an Adult Child Needs to Know

There are seven things every parent of an adult child needs to know, and often no one tells you any of them. I think it would have been nice if someone would have at least mentioned a few of these things *before* my children grew old enough to enter into adulthood. Then I could have prepared myself.

When you are a young parent-to-be, the older and more experienced parents eagerly congratulate you on expecting a child. And then they do it again when your child is born, but this time they also give you advice on early child raising. However, with regard to a child's later adult years, everyone is silent. They only smile knowingly and say nothing about what is ahead. I'm sure they're thinking, *Why say anything now? They'll find out in time.* Or else they believe they are the only ones who are experiencing any challenges with their adult children, so why frighten anyone? Whatever the reason, no one talks about it. At least I never heard anything.

I thought that when your children are 18 they graduate from high school and go to college, and then that is pretty much it for the parenting responsibilities. They have *their* lives and you have *yours,* and they remember everything you taught them, and so they go on to find high paying jobs and get married and come to visit you a few times a year with the grandchildren. Voilà! Parenting season is finished! Now you can do the things you have always dreamed of doing, but were too busy raising children to do.

FORGET IT!

None of that happens!

Your child turns 18 and — you hope — graduates from high school, and then you discover your days of serious parenting are just beginning. You pray he (she) gets into a good college or trade school and that the professors are not teaching him (her) that God is dead and communism is great, or that morality is relative and perversion is to be desired. The influences on your adult child are now more sinister than you ever imagined they would be years ago when he (she) was born — and certainly far more ominous than when you yourself were graduating from high school — and you can't stop thinking about all the frightening possibilities. And while there is *more* to be concerned about, you have *less* control over anything having to do with their lives than ever.

After your children graduate — *if* they graduate — you hope they will find work with some kind of security and benefits. You are always concerned that they will meet someone great to marry, and after they *are* married you hope they will *stay* married. You are concerned about how careful or careless they are with their health and whether they can make the payments on their house. You are concerned about your grandchildren — that you will someday have some and that they will be healthy and raised up to be good, godly children.

Well, I'm here to tell you what you may already be suspecting — or by this time you are certain of it. And I am not just revealing this truth to you — which someone should have told you long ago — I am also giving you a way to handle it. But first I need to share with you SEVEN THINGS EVERY PARENT OF AN ADULT CHILD NEEDS TO KNOW.

1. You Need to Know It Never Ends

The part no one tells you about being a parent is that parenting never stops.

I used to joke with tired, frazzled, and overwhelmed new parents who were worried about the sudden "24-hours-a-day-7-days-a-week responsibility" and the "unending list of things to do with not enough time in a day to do it all" by telling them, "Don't worry. This will only last another 18 years."

I knew that this was a semi-cruel joke, but I wanted them to know the truth. And besides, I loved to hear their weary groans followed by a reluctant laugh. However, I now see that the joke was on *me.* And it is even crueler than I thought. That's because the truth is that it *never ends!* Although there are different stages and seasons of parenting responsibilities, your heart and mind will *always* be with each one of your children for *the rest of your life.* And this is no easy task, for no matter where they go or what they do, a part of you goes with them. When they're happy, you're happy. When they suffer, you suffer. Even after they grow up and you are no longer with them physically on a daily basis, you are still concerned every day — and many *nights,* I might add — about their safety and struggles, their fears and weaknesses, their successes and failures, their choices and mistakes.

Not only is your heart still with your children after they become adults, they are often physically still with *you,* as well.

I remember the day my husband, Michael, and I took our son, Christopher, to college and moved him into his dorm. I cried the entire way back home — which was only about 15 minutes since the university was not far from our house. It wasn't that I would never see him again, but I knew the days of him living with us were over and this was the end of an era. I was feeling sad the next day too, but I busied myself with a writing project that was due; plus I had the company of my 85-year-old dad, who was living with us in the house; my sister, who worked in our home office; and my husband, who was working from home in his studio. At three o'clock that afternoon I heard someone come walking into the house through the back door, and I heard my dad talking to that person.

Who could that be? I wondered. *Everyone who lives or works in the house is here and we aren't expecting anyone.*

I walked into the kitchen, and much to my surprise I saw my son.

"Hey, Christopher. What are you doing back home? Did you forget something?"

"No, I just wanted to say, 'Hi,' " he said cheerfully, and then he sat down at the kitchen table and talked to my dad for nearly two hours. At five o'clock he said goodbye and left to go back to the university to have dinner with his friends on campus and then do some studying.

He did that nearly every day for quite a while, then several times a week, and finally once or twice a week in his junior and senior years. But that first day he came into the kitchen from college was when I began to suspect that it never ends. And it made me smile to think that, of all the places he could go in those two hours in the afternoon, he wanted to be with his family, talking to his grandfather, who was lonely in a house full of workaholics who didn't have time to sit down every day for two hours and talk to him about the old days. My dad lived to be 93, and till the day he died he never stopped talking about how Christopher would come home from college every day just to talk to him.

The truth is, you *never* stop being a parent who deeply cares about your child's well-being, no matter what age they are, what age *you* are, or how close or far away you are from each other. Ever! And not only that, it seems that as adult children, the things they face — or that face *them* — carry even greater consequences than when they were young. And especially far greater consequences than when *you* were young. When we think about how frightening a place the world is, and how rampant and pervasive evil is, and how helpless we feel to do anything about those things, we can drive ourselves crazy with concern.

Although young children can face some very difficult things too — even life-threatening or life-altering situations and conditions — the fact that they are still with us in our homes and under our care and protection makes us feel that we have more control over those situations, or at least more hands-on input for the most part. But when our children are adults and making many decisions on their own without input from us, we see all the possible serious consequences of making the wrong ones. And we also see how *we* will be paying for those wrong decisions right along with them.

When we observe life happening to our adult children in a challenging way, we want to help them. But how much is way overboard, and how little is not enough? Only God knows the answer to that question. We parents of adult children may have many concerns, but not necessarily the opening to do anything about them, or even the opportunity to voice all of our thoughts, suggestions, and opinions. At least not to our adult children. But we do have a grand opening to be able to express those concerns to God and invite *Him* to do something about them. And the greatest thing about that is, when we take our concerns to the Lord — trusting that God hears our prayers and answers them on behalf of our adult children — it means our prayers have power to affect change in their lives. And that gives us a peace we can find no other way.

2. You Need to Know You Can't Fix Them

I had just been introduced to an attractive young woman in her early forties. (When you are my age, 40 is young, 30 is extremely young, and anyone younger than 30 is just a kid.) (For that matter, going the other way, the forties *and* fifties are young, the sixties and seventies are middle-aged, and eighties and above are approaching old age. Maybe in ten years I will revise all that.)

This young woman and I talked briefly about the weather — how hot it was that day and when it was ever going to rain again — and then she abruptly said, "I want to thank you for writing the book . . ."

She couldn't finish the sentence because her lips quivered so much that she had to close her mouth tightly and swallow hard in an attempt to fight back tears. But they refused to be restrained and came streaming down her cheeks anyway.

In the seemingly long moments between when she choked up and when she was finally able to speak again, I wondered if she was hurting in her emotions, or perhaps in her marriage. I touched her arm to comfort her and waited silently until she finally finished her sentence.

". . . your book *The Power of a Praying Parent,*" she said in a trembling voice.

When she said the word "parent," I knew instantly the source of her suffering. It was the kind of deep pain only a parent can feel when something goes wrong with their child. Immediately, countless stories I had heard over the years from other parents came back to me. Their grief over the heartbreak of a child's disobedience, rebellion, sickness, calamities, tragedies, or injuries, or the deep sadness of seeing them not living up to their potential, all came to my mind like a flood.

As it turned out, it was her *adult child* she was talking about. She told me about some of the serious problems she and her husband were having with their 28-year-old son. She said that even the early years with him had been extremely challenging, but that my book helped her through each year and each problem. However, when he became an adult they had to deal with his recklessness, carelessness, laziness, bad choices, bad habits, and numerous personal disasters.

"When does it ever stop?" she sobbed, with tears washing over her face in a steady stream. "How long do we have to keep hurting and suffering and praying for our child and paying for his mistakes — especially financially?"

"I wish I could tell you a definite cutoff date," I answered, "but I don't think there is one. You're not alone in this. I hear these kinds of stories about adult children everywhere I go. Parents are finding it so hard to know where to draw the line between letting an adult child learn a hard lesson, and helping them to get on their feet. We know we can't just give up on them, but sometimes we may have to let them hit bottom. Yet we need to have wisdom about that. We can't stand by and let them destroy themselves, either. We want them to learn the lessons, but we don't want them to ruin their lives in the process. We have to find that balance between pushing them out on eir own before they are ready, and making too easy for them to stay when they need to grow up and learn to fly.

"The only way I know how to discern that fine line between *helping* your adult child and *enabling* him to live a life that is less than what God has for him is to ask the Lord to give you wisdom," I told her. "We all must ask God to show us what to do, and what *not* to do, for our adult children. We have to seek God as to how to pray for them. We need to ask the Lord for clarity and discernment to know when to *just pray* and let Him work in their lives without any other help from us. Only God knows the right thing to do. And only when you have released your adult child completely into God's hands and put the Lord in charge of his life can you ever have true peace. *You* can't change your son, but *God* can. Your son needs you to love him, believe in him, and support him in prayer. And then do whatever it is that the Lord is telling you to do, or *not* do, in order to help him get on the right track."

I prayed with her and her husband, who, as it turned out, was waiting for her just a short distance away from us, and afterward she seemed to have more strength and peace in her soul. I encouraged her to understand that God was the ultimate parent, and He would not only give them wisdom about how to handle their son and his problems, but He would also work in their son's life to change him and his situation and bring him into alignment with God's ways. And God would also take away the guilt they had been feeling about what had been happening with their son.

We all need to understand that we can't "fix" or "change" our adult children. Only God can make changes that last in anyone. Our job is to release our adult children into God's hands and then pray for the Lord to make changes in them and their lives according to His will.

3. You Need to Know God Can Change Everything

It's not easy to be the parent of an adult child. That's because it's difficult to know *what* and *what not* to do for them. When do you need to step in? When have you done too much? When are your expectations too high or too low? When is your tough love too tough or not tough enough? Sometimes you think you are doing the right thing and it isn't. Or maybe it was right for one child but not for another.

I have found that only God can give you

the wisdom you need about those things. And He will give it to you when you ask for it. But first you have to understand and believe that when you pray about your adult child, God will hear and answer. That's the way He set it up. *Prayer is not telling God what to do. Prayer is partnering with God to see that His will is done. You don't have to fully understand what God's will is in order to pray that His will be done.*

You also have to believe that while you cannot change anything in your adult child's life, God can change everything. While it's true that God will not violate someone's strong will, He *will* penetrate someone's heart who is the least bit open to Him. And we never know for sure who is completely closed off to the things of the Lord and who is not. Only God knows that. So we need to pray and let God work. Without our prayers appropriating God's power, our lives are left up to chance with sometimes disastrous results. Let me give you two extreme examples of what I am talking about.

I know of one family — let's call them the Joneses — whose son was continually getting into trouble. He finally got arrested, and instead of bailing him out, Mr. and Mrs. Jones decided to let him learn a hard lesson by leaving him in jail for a while.

Unfortunately, he was assaulted in jail and beaten by one of the prisoners until he was dead from his wounds. The parents got a call from the authorities informing them of what happened and where they could pick up his body. They were devastated and overtaken with guilt because of what they could have prevented. They were good parents who were trying to do the right thing, but it turned out terribly wrong. I don't know where they are today, but I am certain they are still suffering over this tragic event.

I know another family — let's call them the Browns — whose son had also been giving his parents grief for some time. When he got arrested and was sentenced to jail, they also did not try to get him off. They knew he was guilty, and they wanted him to understand the consequences of his behavior. He ended up serving a short time in jail, but it turned his life around. His jail time was such an unforgettably horrible experience that he never wanted to repeat it. All of us who prayed for him asked God to open his eyes to the truth about the path he was on and where he was headed. We prayed that God would reveal to him who he was created to be and the future the Lord had for him. God answered those prayers because he came out a changed person. He went on to college and made something out of his life and didn't waste his time with foolish pursuits again.

Both the Joneses and the Browns were trying to do the right thing — hoping that their actions would inspire total transformation in their adult child. And both sets of parents made basically the same decision. But there were two opposite outcomes. For one family it brought disaster, and for the other it brought redemption. What was the difference? The difference, I believe, was the presence of the Redeemer.

I know for certain that Jesus was invited into the situation of the second family — the Browns. They were believers and the Lord reigned in their hearts. The Holy Spirit was invited to move in this situation with their son, and their friends and they prayed fervently that the Lord would speak to the heart of that young man. In prayer they asked God to pour out His Spirit of truth upon their son and show him what was really happening in his life from God's perspective. In that jail God spoke to his heart, and it became clear to him that although he had done something foolish, he didn't need to continue living like a fool. He had a choice.

To my knowledge, the parents of the first son — the Joneses — were not believers and were not praying people. Their son had not been dedicated to the Lord or taught God's ways or prayed for. He did not have the advantage of the prayers of his parents, family, or friends protecting him and helping him to hear from God in his life. I am not saying that the adult children of parents who pray never have any problems. They definitely do. But if a parent is praying for their adult child, even the bad things that happen will work out in their lives for good. We may not be able to see it at the time, but God will use their situation and turn it into something positive in some way.

God uses what we perceive as problems to get the attention of our adult children and teach them that they cannot live without Him. Sometimes the difficult things that happen to them are really because of the mercy and love of God working in their lives to save them, correct them, or protect them from something far worse (Proverbs 3:11–12).

If you have never prayed for your adult child before, or if some bad things have happened to him or her before you learned how to pray, do not be troubled. God is a Redeemer. Redemption is His specialty. And t only does He redeem our lives from eath and hell and save us for all eternity, He redeems us from hell on earth and saves us in the here and now as well. God will redeem a troubling situation in our lives when He is invited to do so.

When praying for your adult child, there are some things about God you need to believe without a doubt:

1. You must believe that God loves you and your adult children and He will hear your prayers for them. You need to know that "all things work together for good to those who love God, to those who are called according to His purpose" (Romans 8:28). If you love God and want to live His way, then you are called for His purpose. The verses just before that one are talking about prayer. Could it mean that all things work together for good in our lives when we are *praying?*

2. You must believe that God can deliver you from any fears you have about your adult children. What was true for David is true for you as well. David said, "I sought the LORD, and He heard me, and delivered me from all my fears" (Psalm 34:4). You can seek the Lord about your adult children, and He will hear you and deliver you from all your fears as well.

3. You must believe that God can give you

and your adult children what you need wh
you ask for it. You need to have faith i
God's ability to hear and to answer. "Le
him ask in faith, with no doubting, for he who doubts is like a wave of the sea driven and tossed by the wind. For let not that man suppose he will receive anything from the Lord; he is a double-minded man, unstable in all his ways" (James 1:6–8). We can't expect answers to our prayers without having faith in our God to whom we are praying.

4. You must believe that no matter how big your adult child's problems are, God is greater. Jesus said, "The things which are impossible with men are possible with God" (Luke 18:27) and "With God all things are possible" (Matthew 19:26). He also said to one father who was seeking deliverance for his son, "If you can believe, all things are possible to him who believes" (Mark 9:23). He is the God of the impossible, and that means with Him all things are possible. God can change anything or anyone — even you and your adult child — but He must first be invited into the situation. That happens only when you pray.

5. You must believe that because the love and power of God are poured out in you, your prayers for your adult children will always have power. Because your prayers have power, you will always have hope. "Hope does not disappoint, because the love of God has been poured out in our hearts by the Holy Spirit who was given to us" (Romans 5:5). The Holy Spirit is the power of God. When you have the power of God working in your life, you have hope for anything. The list of God's promises to you is far longer than your list of concerns for your adult child.

Every adult child is susceptible to problems. Even the best of children can still experience tough things when they become an adult. Your child may have been dedicated to God or baptized as an infant, received the Lord at two years old, been in Sunday school for 18 years, and have been homeschooled all that time, and yet when he (she) is out from under your control he (she) can still run into some serious challenges, or fall into bad habits, or be exposed to unhealthy influences, or choose undesirable friends, or experience the consequences of wrong choices. But the good news is that God can change all that when you pray.

4. You Need to Know You Must Stop Blaming Yourself

Let's face it. Children are a guilt trip from the time they are born. We find ourselves thinking, *Am I feeding him too much? Am I not feeding her enough? Am I doing too much? Am I not doing enough? Have I given too much? Have I not given enough?* And it's made even more complicated by the fact that every child is different. So what seemed to work for the first child may not work for the second.

Our first child was strong willed, and from the moment Christopher could stand up in his crib he had his mind made up about what he wanted to do and when he wanted to do it, no matter what his parents wanted. It took a lot of strong and consistent discipline in order to get him to see the wisdom of obeying his mom and dad. Our second child was quite different. All it took was an intense look of disapproval if Amanda was doing something wrong, and she would fall apart. Strong discipline for her would have been just as disastrous as weak discipline for him. We always struggled with guilt trying to figure out whether we were coming down too hard on him and not enough on her. Or was it the other way around?

That's not to say we didn't make mistakes

in both directions. Sometimes we were too hard or too easy on each of them. And we saw the consequences of both. We had to ask God for wisdom every day. And I struggled with guilt over all of it — the things I *should* have done or said, but didn't, and the things I *shouldn't* have done or said, but had.

Guilt is a killer. We parents beat ourselves up with guilt every time something bad happens to one of our children because we see how perhaps we could have done things differently and possibly prevented it. For example, if our child doesn't get a good grade in school, we blame ourselves. If she (he) has a problem getting along with a friend, it must somehow be our fault. If she (he) gets sick or injured, we agonize over what we could have done differently to have prevented it. And we do this even more so when they are grown. When we see something in our adult child that we sense is not right, or that violates what we believed we have raised them to be, it makes us wonder, *Where did we go wrong?* When we see something in him or her that is a weakness, we fear we are to blame.

Even if you *have* done something you know has affected your child negatively, you still have to get past it. Perhaps you regret having not been around enough in his or her childhood. Or there were events you missed in your child's life where you know you should have been there. Or you feel you were perhaps too strict or too lenient. Or you said something that you wish you hadn't, or there were things you should have done that you didn't. There is nothing you can do now to erase it or cause it to seem as if it never happened. You have to get beyond it, and that can only be done by the power of the Holy Spirit.

Your first assignment in this book is to get rid of all that guilt!

In order to be effective in praying for your adult child, you must stop blaming yourself for everything that goes wrong. Give God a little credit here. If you have made mistakes, confess them before the Lord — and before your adult child as well, if that will bring healing — so you can enjoy the freedom of forgiveness God has for you. Ask yourself, "Can I do anything about it now?" If so, do it. If not, give it to God and ask Him to redeem the situation and heal you in the process.

This is assuming, of course, that you know the Lord. If you have never received Jesus into your life, ask Him to come into your heart now and forgive you of all your sins d failures and fill you with His Holy pirit. Thank Him that He died on the cross or you so that you can have forgiveness of sins and eternal life with Him forever. Then ask Him to cleanse you from the effects of all past failure and hurt, and help you to live His way now. Ask Him to set you free from guilt.

There are only two ways to avoid guilt as a parent. The first is to die soon after your child is born. The second is to walk with God every day and ask Him for wisdom about everything. I say that walking with God is the better solution of the two. When you walk with God, you can not only go to Him for guidance, you can also ask Him to set you free from any guilt you feel as a parent.

Of course, there are some parents who never blame themselves for anything. Instead, they blame everyone else. They say such things as, "My daughter got into trouble because of the other girls she was with." Or, "My son is lazy because his father never required him to do anything around the house." But the casting of blame on others instead of taking it to God doesn't allow a parent or a child to experience the great good God can bring out of difficult situations. There is so much growth of character when a child is encouraged to see their p… in anything bad they have done.

There are some parents who raise thei… children all the way through high school graduation without a single problem. (At least, I have heard people claiming this has happened to them.) And then problems start after their children go away to college, or after they get their first real job. Or perhaps they *never do* get a real job. Or they don't get a job that lasts longer than a few months. Or they get a job and meet people who are bad influences. Or they marry someone with many problems, and the marriage struggles in every way. Or they marry someone who is very nice, but who is immature and lacks wisdom and good judgment, and so they have one problem after another.

I have seen adult children who appeared to have had perfect lives until they met someone who was an undesirable influence and their lives went downhill from there. Or they got deeply into debt for one reason or another and they needed their parents to bail them out financially. Or they did something stupid and got into trouble and needed their parents to bail them out *literally.*

On the opposite side, I know two parents

ith a child who was difficult to raise all the way through preschool, grade school, middle school, and high school, and then he somehow metamorphosed into a wonderful, productive, and successful adult. But before that metamorphosis happened, these two wonderful Christian parents blamed themselves for all their child's problems.

Perhaps you have raised your child up to be a good and godly person, and yet at times he (she) doesn't live or act as though he (she) has had that kind of upbringing at all. Or perhaps you did not raise your child to trust in God and live His way, and now you feel regret because he (she) has not made godly choices. Or worse yet, your spouse blames you for what's happening and is heaping more guilt on top of the condemnation you already feel. This load is way too heavy for your shoulders to carry. Ask God to help you stop blaming yourself for things that are already done.

Say, "Lord, I can't do anything about what has already happened. Help me to do great things in prayer for my adult children now. Help me to stop blaming myself for everything I see wrong in my adult children's lives. Take away any discouragement I feel."

Remember that discouragement doesn't mean failure. Discouragement is a sign that you need to spend more time with your heavenly Father so He can encourage you.

5. You Need to Know You Have to Forgive

We all must be reminded that unforgiveness can creep into and lurk around the secret corners of our hearts, and we can give place to it without even recognizing what it is. That's why we must periodically ask God to reveal any unforgiveness in us — especially toward our family members.

Forgiveness has to flow *in* us before the power of the Holy Spirit flows *through* us when we pray. The Bible says, "If I regard iniquity in my heart, the Lord will not hear" (Psalm 66:18). One of the greatest iniquities we often harbor in our heart is unforgiveness. That's because it is so easy to do. We can even lie to ourselves and pretend it isn't there. And it's quite easy to hide from others, because even though many people may see it on our face or in our attitude, they usually can't identify what it is. Sometimes we don't see it in ourself because we try so hard to be the good person we know we are, and unforgiveness can be very subtle. But God always sees it, and He doesn't like it. He wants us to get rid of it, and sometimes He will wait to answer our prayers until we do.

Of course we need to forgive everyone, but since I am talking about our adult children here, I have put together a short but important to-do list below for you to check off. I am not trying to torture you; I just want you to be free so your prayers will have power. Remind yourself to forgive the following people and situations. If you have to, write them down as a memo to yourself.

FIRST MEMO TO SELF: *Forgive my adult children for anything they may have done to hurt, disappoint, neglect, or anger me.*

Ask God to show you if you have anything lurking within you that is less than forgiving toward any one of your adult children — and that includes your son-in-law or daughter-in-law as well. It is very important to do this in order to clear the air between you. If they have shown irresponsibility, neglect, rudeness, thoughtlessness, or inconsideration, or they did something that hurt you, confess your feelings about that to the Lord. This is a very subtle thing, because we parents tend to think of ourselves as being far above holding anything against our adult children. We don't like it when we see that kind of thing in others, and we certainly don't want to think of ourselves as entertaining such thoughts. But sometimes these things find a home in our hearts.

Disappointment is another subtle thing we can hold against our adult children anytime they have not lived up to our expectation of them, whether it was warranted or not. By that I mean our expectations may have been too unreasonable for that child, but we still had the expectations and we were disappointed. We have to bring every disappointment before the Lord and give it to Him so that we can completely forgive that adult child for letting us down.

If you don't forgive your adult children for whatever they have done in the past, you may find yourself bringing issues up to them or letting your resentment come out in an unguarded moment. You may also need to *say* something to your adult child about the fact that you are forgiving them for a certain specific thing, but ask God to give you wisdom about that. They may not even know you have held that against them, so there is little good in letting them know now, unless it will clarify something for them that they have sensed, or it will heal something between you.

Don't say words like, "I forgive you for being such an idiot and destroying our family's reputation." Say instead, "I realize I have held the mistakes you made against you, and if I have acted in an unforgiving way toward you, I am very sorry about that and I ask for your forgiveness. I want you to know that I forgive you for all the mistakes of the past, and I ask you to forgive me for all my mistakes too."

Ask God to show you what you need to say, if anything. He will know the perfect timing and He can give you the right words.

And if you ask Him to, He will also prepare your adult child's heart to receive them.

If you have any unforgiveness toward a daughter-in-law or a son-in-law, my advice is to take it to God first long before you take it to them. Get your own heart right with the Lord. This is a very sensitive relationship and a most highly valued one. There is too much at stake and too much room for a terrible misunderstanding that could be disastrous. My advice is to only go to an in-law with a confession on *your* part. For example say, "I need to ask your forgiveness for something I said."

Don't tell a son-in-law or a daughter-in-law that you forgive *them* unless they ask for your forgiveness. For example, don't say to your son-in-law, "I forgive you for taking my daughter away and ruining her life." And don't say to a daughter-in-law, "I forgive you for spending all my son's money so that he has to struggle to make ends meet." Remember that you do want to see your grandchildren some day.

Forgiving your adult children is very important for everyone concerned. Ask God to help you. Ask Him to reveal anything you might not be seeing. If you feel your adult children should ask *you* for forgiveness, pray that they will be able to do that. However, don't wait around for it. You start moving on what *you* know to do and pray for it to happen in their hearts as well.

SECOND MEMO TO SELF: *Forgive my adult child's other parent.*

It is very likely that most of us can see something in the other parent of our adult child that we would have liked to see changed. This may be something that has affected your child in a negative way. If you see some weakness or character flaw in your adult child for which you blame your spouse, ask God to help you forgive your husband (wife) and let go of it for good. Ask God to cleanse your heart so you can be free to move on. What is done is done, and you need to be free to start praying for your adult child with a clean heart now. I have always said, and have written it in all my books, that *forgiving someone doesn't make the other person right; it makes you free.* You *have* to get free.

If you are praying for an adult stepchild, ask God to help you have a forgiving heart toward his or her other parents. Anything you see wrong in that adult child can easily be blamed on them, and resentment can build up in your heart over it. No matter what has gone on in the past, it is time to let it all go. The consequences of not forgiving are just too serious to allow it to continue.

Again, this kind of unforgiveness may be hard to detect. If the feelings have been around for a long time, they may be so much a part of you that you don't even see them. That's why you have to ask God to show you. Say, "Lord, show me if I have any unforgiveness or resentment in me toward the other parent (or parents) of my adult child." You will be amazed at how fast God will answer that prayer.

THIRD MEMO TO SELF: *Forgive anyone in my adult child's past whom I believe did harm to him or her in any way.*

I remember an adult coach who humiliated one of my young children one time and the memory of it hurt both me and my child. It was entirely out of order and uncalled for, and it was done in front of teammates and their parents. It was a cruel thing to do, and I believe it was done out of a jealous spirit in that coach. But I had to bring it before the Lord a number of times in order to get it out of my heart and mind.

Years later when my child was an adult, I had to pray about it all over again because I saw things in that child that I thought were a direct result of the incident. I prayed, "Lord, I lift the memory of that hurtful incident to You and confess that it still irritates me. But more importantly, I feel it created a hurt in my child that has carried over for years, and perhaps the effects of it are still felt. I don't want to carry it around in me any longer, and I certainly don't want my adult child to carry it either. I forgive that coach for those hurtful words. Change my attitude toward that person. Most of all, heal my adult child's heart and fill it with complete forgiveness for that person and that incident."

Ask God to show you if there is anything from the past that happened to your child that still haunts you and makes you feel anything at all negative. You have to get rid of it because it is cluttering up your mind and may be interfering with your ability to pray effectively.

Fourth Memo to Self: *Forgive myself for anything in the past where I felt I could have done better as a parent.*

Ask God to show you where you have any regrets regarding the raising of your children. If there are things you are still kicking yourself for, or if you cringe when you think about what you wish you would have said or done — or wished you had *not* said or done — then bring those things before the Lord. Ask Him to forgive you and help you to forgive yourself. Tell Him you want to have a clean heart so you can make a fresh start as a praying parent of an adult child. If you don't get free of this, the enemy of your soul will always be using it against you.

If you have made mistakes — and let's just assume *we all* have — ask God to redeem them. Even if you have walked with God and tried to live His way, but fear that you have made mistakes in raising your child, bring them before God now. Don't waste another moment of your life with guilt and condemnation on your shoulders. Say, "Lord, I confess I feel regret and guilt about some things I did or did not do as a parent. (Confess any specifics that are on your heart.) Help me to let go of the past and not look backward, but move forward with You."

Ask God to give you the ability to also *apologize* to your children when it is warranted. Your adult children need to hear the words "Forgive me" as much as you do. This will free them as well. If they need to forgive *you* for anything, they will be stuck where they are and unable to move forward in their lives until they do.

Once you have confessed all that and your heart is clean before the Lord, know that any condemnation you feel from now on will be coming from the enemy of your soul. And that's where the blame should be placed.

These brief memos you just read are extremely important. Don't neglect any of these four areas of forgiveness, because each one of them can hinder the answers to your prayers.

6. You Need to Know There Is Only One Perfect Parent

Let's get something straight. There are no perfect parents. That's because no person on earth is perfect. There has only ever been one perfect parent, and that is our Father God. You and I are His adult children. And you know how much trouble He has had raising us. But He is always there waiting for us to come to our senses and do things His way. Because He is the best parent, He is the only one who can really help us to be the best parent to our adult children. We have to learn from Him.

The Bible says to "train up a child in the way he should go, and when he is old he will not depart from it" (Proverbs 22:6). That's great news for those who trained their children in the ways of God right from early childhood. But what about all the parents who didn't know the Lord and His ways at the time they were raising their children, and so their adult children are not walking in God's ways now? Is it too late for them?

What about those of us who *did* know the Lord when we were raising our children, and were walking in the ways of the Lord the best we knew how, but were still less than perfect parents? Can those of us who look back wishing we could do some things over again, knowing what we know now, ever have a chance to make up for lost time?

I don't believe it's ever too late for any of us who know the Lord. That's because God is a Redeemer, and it is never too late to see Him work amazing redemption in response to our prayers — especially prayers for our adult children.

If you have not walked with God through your early parenting years and your child is an adult now, go before God and confess that to Him. Say, "Lord, I confess that I did not know You, or live Your way, or seek You when I was bringing up my child. Forgive me for any mistakes I have made. Help me to make up for it by living Your way now. Show me how to pray for my adult child the way You would have me to."

I am certain that through our prayers, and His love and mercy, God can teach our children the things we didn't. That's why I chose the Scripture in the front of the book that talks about this. In this passage God is speaking to His people — through Isaiah the prophet — words of hope and promises of restoration. He says as surely as the promise He made "that the waters of Noah would no longer cover the earth," He also promises that "the mountains shall depart and the hills be removed, but My kindness shall not depart from you" (Isaiah 54:9–10). He says of these promises that this is the "heritage of the servants of the Lord" (verse 17). In the midst of these many promises is the promise that every parent should keep close to their heart: "All your children shall be taught by the Lord, and great shall be the peace of your children" (verse 13).

What a great promise to all of God's people!

We are still benefiting from the promise about the floodwaters never again rising on earth as they did in Noah's time. And God says the promise that He will teach our children is just as sure as that one. That's why we can claim these promises for our adult children. However, just because we understand something in the Word of God to be a promise for us doesn't mean it just happens automatically. We *must pray* about it. Pray that your understanding of the promises in God's Word will bring added faith to pray and believe for their realization in your life.

Assuming that you and I and have done the best we knew how at the time we raised our children, and knowing that we were not perfect parents, we can trust that our children can still be taught by the Lord today and for the rest of their lives. They can learn the things we didn't teach them — or didn't teach them as well as we should have — and they can unlearn the things we taught them that were not so good. Did we teach them how to fight with their spouse because we fought with ours? Did we teach them that adults are too busy for their children, so then they will be too busy for theirs? Did we teach them that they don't have to work hard for anything because we made it too easy for them to get everything they wanted? Did we teach them that they don't need to go to church because that is what we modeled for them? Whatever wasn't perfect about the way we taught our children, God can redeem all that and teach them what they need to know now. But we need to pray for that to happen.

7. You Need to Know You Can Wholeheartedly Say, "For This Adult Child I Prayed"

Five of those six words in quotes above were spoken by Hannah in the Bible, who had prayed and prayed for a son. Hannah "was in bitterness of soul, and prayed to the LORD and wept in anguish" (1 Samuel 1:10) over the lack of a child. Then she vowed to the Lord that if He would give her a son, she would give him to the Lord for all of his life. The Lord heard her prayer, and she gave birth to a son the following year.

When the child was about three, Hannah took him to the temple and presented him to the Lord as she promised. She said to the priest, "*For this child I prayed,* and *the* LORD *has granted me my petition* which I asked of Him. Therefore, I also have *lent him to the* LORD*;* as long as he lives he shall be lent to the LORD" (1 Samuel 1:27–28, emphasis added). And then she worshipped God. Notice the words in italics. *For this child I prayed . . . the* LORD *has granted my petition . . . I have also lent him to the* LORD*.* Keep those words in mind as you read this book.

Hannah's story is one of the greatest examples of a parent's fervent and unrelenting prayers. It has been my observation in the Word, and in life, that the more fervent the prayers, the more amazing the things God will do through them. That's why I don't want you to become *discouraged* when you are praying for your adult child. I want you to become *fervent.* The result of Hannah's fervent, longtime prayers was that she gave birth to Samuel, who became one of the greatest and most influential and powerful leaders in all of Israel.

You never know what wonderful and great things you will give birth to in your fervent prayers for your adult child. But first you must do what Hannah did and commit your adult child to the Lord. You have to release your child into God's hands. All through the Old Testament and into the New Testament are examples of parents presenting their children to the Lord. It is important to do that as early as possible. It must be clear to all — especially the enemy — that this child is the Lord's. If you have never done that, you can do it now. Say, "Lord, I present (name of adult child) to You. I dedicate him (her) to You for Your glory. Even though I see from Your Word that it is good to have done this from infancy, I also know from Your Word that it is never too late to do the right thing. I release him (her) into Your hands now."

If you have already dedicated your child to God, say, "Lord, I rededicate (name of adult child) to You. I pray she (he) will serve You all the days of her (his) life and that she (he) will glorify You in every way. As long as she (he) lives, I pray she (he) will be under Your watchful eye. I again release her (him) into Your hands. In Jesus' name I pray."

Then worship God, as Hannah did, and give glory to Him who is greater than anything you or your adult child faces now or will ever face in the future. Thank God for all the great gifts God has put into her (him). Praise Him for the wonderful things He is going to do in her (his) life through your prayers.

The only way to have peace about your adult child is to know that you have covered her (him) in prayer. When you can say as Hannah did, "For this child I prayed," then you will know that you have done the greatest thing you can do for her (him). When you can say, "The Lord has answered my prayer," you will have joy in your soul. And when you have released your adult children to the Lord, you will have peace knowing you have put them into your heavenly Father's hands, who is the greatest parent of all.

Understanding that your job as a parent never ends doesn't have to be an overwhelming burden. It can be a rewarding challenge. God has given you charge over each of your adult children to cover them in prayer, and to love and support them in any way that you and the Lord see fit to do. It is a privilege to serve the Lord in this way, knowing you are working with Him to see that these precious children of His are not lost, destroyed, or lured off the path and away from the blessings He has for them. And this is true no matter what age they are. I know people in their eighties and nineties who are praying for their adult children who are in their sixties and seventies. Remember that I said it never ends?

Even if you have an adult child who has strayed off the path God has for him (her) — or who has never been on the right path to begin with — know that your prayers can help him (her) hear from God and be able to make wise choices and end up where he (she) is supposed to be. While God won't violate the will of your adult child, your prayers still have a strong influence in his (her) life. Your prayers can open doors that need to be opened and close doors that need to be closed.

If you are just starting to pray for your adult child, it takes a while to turn that ship around and head it in a new direction. Keep on praying no matter what happens, and don't give up. While there are no guarantees when it comes to the outcome of actions born of human wisdom, there *are* guarantees when it comes to prayer and the heart of God. If you are praying to the God of the impossible for an adult child who is himself (herself) impossible — or who seems to be in an impossible situation — this means you will have the opportunity to witness a miracle.

We no longer have control over our adult children. We can't make them do what *we* want. But by praying, we can help them to hear from God so He can lead them to do what *He* wants. By our prayers we can help them avoid the pitfalls of life and the traps of the enemy designed for their destruction. It's not that we are trying to pray every problem away from them — even if that were possible — for then they would never grow up and learn the lessons they need to learn. But we can help them stay on the right path so they can rise up to become all they were created to be.

We don't always know the specific details of what we need to pray about for our adult children, because often they only let us know what they want us to know. But when we *do* know specific things to pray about concerning their lives, by all means we should pray about those things. However, there is a way to pray every day for your adult children, without knowing any specifics, that will cover their lives and keep them on the path God has for them.

The next 14 chapters contain 14 ways to pray for your adult children, no matter what is happening in their lives. Whether their lives are perfect, or everything is going wrong, or somewhere in between, praying about these things will protect them, get them moving in the right direction, and give you peace in the process. The first four chapters are a crucial foundation for the rest, so read these in order so you can lay the foundation. Then you can move through the other ten chapters in any order you want, according to your greatest concerns.

Because no one has the burden of heart for your adult children that you do, your prayers for them will have a fervency that no one else's will have. Shall we get started?

Prayer Power

Lord, I pray You would teach me how to intercede for my adult children. Thank You that You love me and my children and You will hear my prayers for them. Set me free from all worry and concern I have about them so I can have peace. I know You are greater than anything they face. Thank You that because Your love and power are poured out in me, my prayers for them will have power.

Help me to not blame myself for things that go wrong in their lives. Where I have made mistakes I confess those to You and ask that You would redeem them all and release me from guilt. Help me to forgive my adult children for anything they have done to hurt or disappoint me. Help me to forgive my adult children's other parent for anything I feel he or she did wrong in raising them. Help me to forgive anyone who has hurt my adult children in any way. Help me to forgive myself for any time I feel that I have not been the perfect parent.

Lord, I know You are the only perfect parent. Thank You for loving my adult children as much as I do. Thank You for hearing my prayers for them. Give me faith to believe and patience to wait for the answers. Today I say, "For this adult child I prayed, and

You, Lord, have heard my prayers and granted my petition" (1 Samuel 1:27). I give You all praise and glory.

In Jesus' name I pray.

Word Power

This is the confidence that we have in Him, that if we ask anything according to His will, He hears us. And if we know that He hears us, whatever we ask, we know that we have the petitions that we have asked of Him.
1 John 5:14–15

My soul, wait silently for God alone, for my expectation is from Him.
Psalm 62:5

Ask, and it will be given to you; seek, and you will find; knock, and it will be opened to you. For everyone who asks receives, and he who seeks finds, and to him who knocks it will be opened.
Matthew 7:7–8

To Him who is able to do exceedingly abundantly above all that we ask or think, according to the power that works in us, to Him be glory in the church by Christ Jesus to all generations, forever and ever.
Ephesians 3:20–21

Continue earnestly in prayer, being vigilant in it with thanksgiving.
Colossians 4:2

1
Pray That Your Adult Children Will See God Pour Out His Spirit upon Them

Once you have released your adult children into God's hands and dedicated — or rededicated — their lives to Him (as I described near the end of the introduction), then the first and most important way to start praying is to ask God to pour out His Spirit upon them. It doesn't matter what else you need to pray about specifically; you will be heading upstream against a strong current if you and they are not moving with the flow of God's Spirit.

Every day we want the Spirit of God to come upon us and carry us where we need to go. We want Him to open our eyes to the truth and open our ears to hear His voice. We want Him to fill us afresh with His Spirit so that our lives can be lived for Him and we can move into all He has for us. And that is exactly what we want for our adult children as well.

Ideally, our adult children will ask for an

outpouring of the Holy Spirit themselves. But realistically, many young people don't even think about doing that, or understand what it means or why they should. It would be wonderful if our adult children would pray for *all* the things suggested in this book over their own lives, but whether they do or don't, they still need our prayer support.

Pray That They Will Welcome an Outpouring of the Holy Spirit

A glorious promise God proclaimed to His people was first heard in the Old Testament through the prophet Joel (Joel 2:28) and then quoted later in the New Testament by Peter. It says:

> "It shall come to pass in the last days, says God, that *I will pour out of My Spirit on all flesh; your sons and your daughters shall prophesy,* your young men shall see visions, your old men shall dream dreams" (Acts 2:17, emphasis added).

We are living in the last days God is talking about. If you are not sure about that, read your Bible and then turn on the TV and watch it for a week. You will see unmistakable signs of it everywhere. The promise for our adult children in the words "your sons and your daughters shall prophesy" is that, when the Holy Spirit is poured out on them, they will be able to hear from God. They will have a word from God in their hearts, and it will become the motivating factor in their lives. And God will be glorified in the process.

When our adult children can hear from God, then they will know where He is leading them, and they will understand how He wants them to serve Him. They may not know specifics, but they will have direction. Too often young adults can't figure out the direction for their lives because they haven't heard a word in their hearts from God about it. This can carry on for years until you have adult children who are aimless and don't feel any sense of purpose or calling. But when the Holy Spirit is poured out upon them, they can sense direction from God, and He is able to lead them on the right paths and secure their steps in ways they couldn't begin to do on their own.

I have known too many good, godly, believing parents who had an adult child who did nothing for years after he (she) graduated from high school. In each case he (she) refused to go to a college or a trade school and couldn't or wouldn't find a job. The parents prayed and prayed and threatened and prodded and begged to no effect. Then one day, after they had prayed that God would pour out His Spirit upon him (her), their adult child got up off the couch, turned off the TV, and went out and made a life for himself (herself).

You might be thinking, *Why didn't those parents just throw their lazy adult children out?* But it is not as easy as it sounds. When you throw them out they can get into a lot of trouble. They can become more vulnerable to evil influences because they are afraid or desperate. You must have the mind of God about this. You have to be certain that throwing your adult child out of your house is what God wants you to do. In some cases it may well be, but it can't be a decision born of human emotions, such as anger. I know some parents who shipped their adult child out because they thought it would do him good, and it turned out to be a terrible decision because he fell under some horrible influences.

We have to keep in mind that *God* can do far more for our adult children than *we* can ever do, and so we must ask *Him* to speak to their hearts by the power of His Holy Spirit. They need to be able to hear from God regarding every aspect of their lives, from decisions they make about where they go and what they do to the people they spend time with and perhaps try to emulate.

Some adult children are going to be more open to hearing from God and receptive to the move of His Spirit in their lives than others. Some will not be open or receptive at all. At least not at first. Whether they are open or not shouldn't affect your prayers. You pray what needs to be prayed regardless of what your adult child's attitude is toward the things of God. *Your* job is to pray, and it is *God's* job to answer. Remember, you have released your adult child into God's hands. That doesn't mean you have given up on him or her. You're not saying, "You take him, God. I can't deal with him anymore." Or, "That's it, Lord. I've had it. She's all Yours now." It means you have surrendered the burden you have been carrying for your adult child to the Lord so He can take it off of your shoulders. Then the burden you carry is in prayer.

Pray That They Will Understand the Power of the Holy Spirit

I wrote *The Power of a Praying Parent* more than 15 years ago, and it has served me and others well in all those years. I have seen countless answers to prayer in my own children's lives, and I have heard from thousands of readers about the wonderful answers to prayer they have experienced as well. Those of us who started praying for our small children back then have seen them grow into adults. And we have also watched the world change for the worse in some way every day. We must now have a new strategy in prayer for our adult children. Our prayers for the flow of the Holy Spirit in their lives will become a powerful protective shield from the flood of this toxic culture. They cannot navigate it successfully without God's power.

Today's cultural environment will chew our adult children up and spit them out if they are not strong enough to recognize the destructive, dark, and powerful forces that are in it and be able to resist them. No matter how horrible our own background might have been, we weren't confronted with the outpouring of evil they are facing today. It is becoming so dangerous that even our adult children cannot successfully withstand it on their own. They need the power of the Holy Spirit, and they need our prayers to help them understand how He moves in power on their behalf.

We must not only *politely ask* God for an outpouring of His Spirit on our adult children, we must get on our knees and *cry out* for it from the depths of our being. We must recognize that already a spirit is being poured out on them right now — the spirit of darkness, death, perversion, lies, destruction, and evil — and only an outpouring of the Holy Spirit can negate that in their lives before it harms or destroys them. Only an outpouring of the Holy Spirit can connect them to the power of God.

Pray That They Will Be Influenced by the Holy Spirit of Truth

The Holy Spirit is the Spirit of truth (John 16:13). We all must have Him functioning in that capacity fully in our lives. And this is especially true for our adult children. The Spirit of truth will bring the truth to light and expose the lies.

I am deliberately not telling many stories about my own adult children in this book, and that is not because there aren't any stories to tell. But Christopher and Amanda are adults, and these are *their* stories to tell. And I hope that someday they will, for the outcome in each case has been great to the glory of God. However, I will say that each one of my adult children at one point presented us with a challenge that made it necessary to confront them about some choices they had made with regard to the path they were on. They each had gotten off the path God had for them because of bad influences in their lives. I am not blaming the bad influences, because obviously something in each adult child allowed them to be drawn toward what they clearly knew was not right.

This happened in separate years and ages for each of them, and they were dealing with entirely different issues. However, in both cases I had previously sensed in *my* spirit that something was not quite right in *their* spirits. A parent can look into their adult child's eyes and see if the Holy Spirit is reflected back in all His purity, or if something has come into their mind and soul that is competing with His presence. And this is especially true when you ask the Holy Spirit of truth to reveal what you need to know in order to pray effectively for their lives.

My husband and I felt something was not right, but we didn't have any hard evidence. So we just prayed that God would reveal everything that needed to be revealed, and that He would not let them get away with anything. We asked God to pour out His Spirit upon them and convict them of whatever was in their lives that was not glorifying to Him. We asked the Spirit of truth to reveal the truth to them and to us.

In each case, not long after we prayed, someone called us to say they were concerned about our adult child and why. We went to each one and told them what the Holy Spirit had put on our hearts. We also told them what we had heard, although not whom we heard it from. (I never reveal my sources.) They each immediately admitted to what we suspected and were deeply and completely repentant.

This was a turning point for each adult child, because they were different from then on. They were more serious about their lives, their futures, and the Lord. They became far more careful and wise about their associations and actions. The Holy Spirit spoke powerfully to them, and their hearts were opened to a new level of His work in their lives. All this could not have happened without the Spirit of truth penetrating their lives and revealing what they needed to see.

Even though I am not using many stories from my own adult children's lives — except in a few minor instances such as this, where their privacy is not compromised — there are countless parents of adult children with whom I have talked at great length about the problems they have faced with their adult children. These conversations have given me more than enough examples to illustrate what I need to in each chapter. However, so as to protect everyone's privacy, I will not mention any real names or specifics that would allow someone to be identified. Plus, nearly every example I am citing is based on more than one case. So it could be any one of a number of adult children whom I am talking about in this book.

All that to say, I have seen countless answers to prayers for adult children. Were I to tell you all of them, you would be greatly encouraged in praying for your own. I hope the ones I mention will give you the encouragement you need.

If you have an adult child who has grieved or worried you, or caused problems for himself (herself) or for you or others, ask God to pour out His Spirit on him (her) right now. Don't waste time blaming yourself, the other parent, or your child. I am not saying your adult children don't bear any responsibility for what happens in their lives. They certainly do. But the overriding factor is that only an outpouring of the Holy Spirit of God on your adult children is powerful enough to withstand the onslaught of the spirit of evil coming against them. Asking God to pour out His Spirit upon your adult children is a simple prayer with powerful ramifications, both for you and for them.

I have asked God to pour out His Holy Spirit on *you* and speak to your heart as you pray for an outpouring of the Holy Spirit on your adult children. I can't wait to hear about the results.

Lord, You have said that in the last days You will pour out Your Spirit upon all flesh. I cry out to You from the depth of my heart and ask that You would pour out Your Holy Spirit upon my adult children. Pour out Your Spirit upon me and my other family members as well. Pour out Your Spirit on all of their in-laws, both present and future. Pour out Your Spirit upon whatever difficult circumstances each of my adult children are facing. Be Lord over every part of their lives and every aspect of their being.

Speak to my adult child's heart and help him (her) to hear from You. Enable him (her) to understand Your leading and direction for his (her) life. Open his (her) ears to hear Your truth so he (she) will reject all lies. Help him (her) to move by the power of Your Spirit. Enable him (her) to rise above the onslaught of evil in our culture.

Where he (she) has walked away from You in any way, stretch out Your hand and draw him (her) back. Don't let him (her) get away with anything that is not pleasing in Your sight. Convict his (her) heart and bring him (her) back to where he (she) should be. May the Holy Spirit poured out on him (her) completely neutralize the power of the enemy attempting to pour out evil in his (her) life.

I know You can do far more in my adult child's life than I can ever do, and I invite You to do so. But if there is anything I should do — or should *not* do — make it clear to me so that I will do the right thing. Holy Spirit of truth, reveal the truth that needs to be seen both to them and to me. Guide me in my response to them always.

I pray my adult child will never grieve Your Holy Spirit (Ephesians 4:30) but will receive Him as a gift from You (Luke 11:13). Fill him (her) with Your Spirit and pour into him (her) Your peace, hope, faith, truth, and power. Let a spirit of praise arise in his (her) heart and teach him (her) to worship You in Spirit and in truth.

In Jesus' name I pray.

WORD POWER

If you then, being evil, know how to give good gifts to your children, how much more will your heavenly Father give the Holy Spirit to those who ask Him!

LUKE 11:13

You shall receive power when the Holy Spirit has come upon you.

ACTS 1:8

Anyone who speaks a word against the Son of Man, it will be forgiven him; but whoever speaks against the Holy Spirit, it will not be forgiven him, either in this age or in the age to come.

MATTHEW 12:32

Prophecy never came by the will of man, but holy men of God spoke as they were moved by the Holy Spirit.

2 PETER 1:21

Repent, and let every one of you be baptized in the name of Jesus Christ for the remission of sins; and you shall receive the gift of the Holy Spirit.

ACTS 2:38

2
Pray That Your Adult Children Will Develop a Heart for God, His Word, and His Ways

People who have a heart for God want to know Him. And they want to know Him well. People who seek after God want what *He* wants. And what God wants is that we become more like Him. Because we all fall short of the standard God has for us in the way we think, act, and live our lives, we all need to change. But only God can make changes in us that last. And only as we seek Him for those changes.

No matter how long we have known God or walked with Him, we can always pray we will know Him better and walk with Him closer. In the same way we pray for ourselves, we can also pray for our adult children. While we can't pray a relationship with God into existence for them, we *can* pray that their hearts will be *turned toward the Lord* and open to *receive from Him.* We can pray that they have a *desire to know God better* and to *become more like Him.* We can pray that their hearts will be closed to the lies of the enemy and open to God's truth.

Below are some specific ways to pray about your adult child's walk with God.

Pray That They Desire to Know God

A desire in any person's heart to know God will be the thing that saves his life. That's because anyone who truly wants to know God is going to eventually be led to the feet of Jesus, the Savior. There may be others in the world who claim they can save you, but Jesus is the only one who died and rose again to prove that *He* is the one who really can.

We all need to be saved because we are lost without Christ. The apostle Peter said of Jesus, "Nor is there salvation in any other, for there is no other name under heaven given among men by which we must be saved" (Acts 4:12). Without Jesus we will wander around trying to find a place for ourselves in this world and never really succeed. We will always feel there is something missing because we won't have the solid connection to God and His power we need in order to survive. And our *eternal* future will not be good.

We all need to be saved because that is the only way we can become new. "If anyone is in Christ, he is a new creation; old things have passed away; behold, all things have become new" (2 Corinthians 5:17). We all need to have a new beginning. Some of us feel that we need one every day. There is only one way to truly experience becoming new, and that is by having Christ living in us and renewing us.

There is no adult child so good that they have no need of being saved. And there is no adult child so bad that they *cannot* be saved. The Bible says that God did not forsake the Israelites even "though their land was filled with sin against the Holy One of Israel" (Jeremiah 51:5). If God did not forsake His people after all the terrible things they did, He is not going to forsake your adult child no matter what she (he) has done, either. And especially not when there is a fervently praying mom or dad such as yourself knocking on heaven's door every day in intercession. Your prayers can help your adult child open her (his) heart to God and better hear from Him.

Your adult child may have known the Lord from an early age, and if that is so, continue to pray that she (he) never falls away from Him. And don't think it can't happen to you, because every believer is the devil's target, and he doesn't give up trying to get us off the path. There are influences in the world today designed specifically for that purpose. Your adult child needs your prayers in order to stay strong in the battle.

If your adult child does not know the Lord, pray that she (he) has an encounter with the living God. Though it is hard to imagine, God cares even more about her (his) salvation than you do. "The Lord is not slack concerning His promise, as some count slackness, but is longsuffering toward us, not willing that any should perish but that all should come to repentance" (2 Peter 3:9).

In the Bible God showed the prophet Jeremiah two baskets of figs. One of the baskets had *good* figs ready for eating; the other contained *bad* figs that were inedible. God said that just as bad figs couldn't be eaten because they were so bad, bad people were just as useless and He would "deliver them to trouble" and their lives would be cursed with one problem after another (Jeremiah 24:8–10). The bad people He is talking about here are people whose hearts are hard against God and everything He stands for.

On the other hand, God said the *good* figs were like the good people who had been carried away captive at that time. God said

He had *allowed* them to be taken away, but He would keep His eye on them and bring them back and build them up. He would plant them so they could bear fruit, and not pluck them up so they would be destroyed (Jeremiah 24:1–6).

What this says to me about the nature of God with regard to our adult children is that when a person is hard-heartedly sold out to opposing God in every way, God will give him or her over to trouble. But with someone who has a heart to *know God,* He will watch over them and build them up so that they can become fruitful. And even though they may get off the path and God may allow some difficult things to happen to them, it will be for their own ultimate good.

The next thing God says about the good people who are represented by the good figs is, "Then *I will give them a heart to know Me,* that I am the LORD; and they shall be My people, and I will be their God, for *they shall return to Me with their whole heart*" (Jeremiah 24:7, emphasis added).

Thank God for that wonderful promise to us and especially to our adult children! *Even though they may have walked away from God, He will give them a heart to know Him.* And if they have ended up a long way from where they are supposed to be, God will use it for good and cause them to wholeheartedly return to Him.

This promise alone should give any parent hope. The thing about the promises of God, however, is that they must be bathed in prayer in order to appropriate them for our lives. We must say, "Lord, I pray that You will give (name of adult child) a heart to know You as Lord, and that she (he) will always turn to You with her (his) whole heart."

Pray That They Desire to Live God's Way

One of the many reasons to pray that God will pour out His Spirit upon our adult children is that having the Holy Spirit in our lives is the only way we can live God's way successfully. We all need help with that. No one can obey God's laws perfectly without God's help. We can't make ourselves good enough to have a relationship with God. When we give our hearts and lives to God, *He* helps us to be obedient and good. The *choice* is ours, but *He* makes it happen.

Jesus said He had to go away in order to send the Holy Spirit to us. "I tell you the truth. It is to your advantage that I go away; for if I do not go away, the *Helper* will not come to you; but if I depart, I will send Him to you. And when He has come, *He will convict the world of sin,* and of righteousness, and of judgment" (John 16:7–8, emphasis added). The Holy Spirit is too pure to reside in people who are not themselves purified. We are purified by the blood of Jesus, the sacrificial Lamb of God. When we receive Jesus, we are purified by the blood He shed on our behalf when He paid the penalty for our sins.

The Holy Spirit is the only one who can help us do the right thing. He teaches us what to do by speaking to our hearts and breathing life into the Word of God as we learn from it. He also works in our hearts a propensity to do the right thing. He forms in us a holy barometer that tells us instinctively what is right or wrong. The Bible says that when we live according to the Spirit, we set our minds on the things of the Spirit. It says that we are *in* the Spirit if the Spirit of God dwells *in* us (Romans 8:6–10). But God doesn't knock down the door to our hearts. He waits to be invited. While we cannot pray the Holy Spirit into our adult children, we *can* pray for a softening of their hearts and an opening to hear the Lord's voice speaking to them. We *can* pray for a silencing of the enemy's lies around them, so that they can hear the voice of the Spirit of truth.

No one can know what God's ways are if they don't read His Word. Pray for your adult child to have a heart for God's Word. The Bible says that God's laws are "perfect, converting the soul" . . . "sure, making wise the simple" . . . "right, rejoicing the heart" . . . "pure, enlightening the eyes" . . . "more to be desired . . . than gold" . . . and "sweeter also than honey and the honey-comb" (Psalm 19:7–10). The book of Proverbs says, "*He who despises the Word will be destroyed,* but he who fears the commandment will be rewarded" (Proverbs 13:13, emphasis added). The last thing we want is for our adult children to be destroyed for lack of knowledge of God's Word and His ways.

We all must have knowledge of the truth, which is the Word of God, so that we won't end up believing a lie. "Do not listen to the words of the prophets who prophesy to you. They make you worthless; they speak a vision of their own heart, not from the mouth of the LORD . . . and to everyone who walks according to the dictates of his own heart, they say, 'No evil shall come upon you' " (Jeremiah 23:16–17). How many people have been led on a path to destruction because they believed a lie and not the truth? Pray that your adult children will have such great knowledge of the truth that they will spot a lie of the enemy a mile away. Pray that they will not listen to people who speak a vision of their own hearts. Any person who follows people who despise the Lord will himself be led astray and destroyed.

If you did not raise your children in the ways of God because you did not know the Lord or His ways, ask God to redeem that situation now. Thank Him for all the ways you taught your children that *were* right and good. Remember that He said, "All your children will be taught by the Lord," so ask Him to teach your adult children His ways every day.

If you raised your children in the ways of God and they have strayed from them as adults, pray that they will no longer turn their backs on Him. God says of people who do not listen to His instruction, "*They have turned to Me the back,* and not the face; though I taught them, rising up early and teaching them, yet they have not listened to receive instruction" (Jeremiah 32:33, emphasis added). Pray that your adult children will listen to the voice of God and never turn their backs on Him.

If you are one of the blessed parents whose adult children were raised in the ways of God, and they have never strayed from them, pray that they never will. God said, "They shall be My people, and I will be their God; then I will give them one heart and one way, that they may fear Me forever, *for the good of them* and *their children after them.* And I will make an everlasting covenant with them, that *I will not turn away from doing them good; but I will put My fear in their hearts so that they will not depart from Me*" (Jeremiah 32:38–40, emphasis added).

Pray for your adult children to always have the fear of God in their hearts. Thank Him that the fear of God in *your* heart will become a rich inheritance for *them* as well.

Pray That They Desire to Have a Repentant Heart

Having a repentant heart is one of the keys to success. A repentant heart says, "Show me my sins, Lord, and I will repent of them. Lead me in Your ways. I will not rebelliously cling to *my* way of doing things if it is against *Your* ways." Having a repentant heart doesn't mean we have necessarily done something terrible, although it can mean that. What it means is that we are willing to let God show us if we have not done things perfectly. It means we are open to seeing our own errors instead of self-righteously thinking we are so good that we never need to repent of anything.

In my book *The Power of Prayer to Change Your Marriage,* I talk about how, in many of the marriages I have seen that have broken down and ended in divorce, there was always at least one person who did not have a repentant heart. There was one person who would not say, "I see my part in these problems and I will do what it takes to rectify it." Actually, both people should be saying that and not just one. Often, a woman had been asking for some kind of change in her husband, and he refused to listen. He refused to see what he needed to do to accommodate her wishes. He refused to have a repentant heart. The repentant heart is the key. And God will give that to any person who seeks to have it.

A repentant heart is one in which there is no rebellion. Rebellion says, "I want what I want when I want it, and I deserve to have it no matter how I get it or whom I hurt. I don't have to live by the rules. I don't have to live by my *parents'* rules, I don't have to live by *God's* rules, and I don't have to live by my *spouse's* rules. I have *my own rules* and other people live by mine." Rebellion is deliberately living outside of the Lord's ways.

Jeremiah talked to God about Israel being disobedient to the Lord's ways and receiving judgment, saying, "O LORD, are not Your eyes on the truth? You have stricken them, but they have not grieved; You have consumed them, but they have refused to receive correction. They have made their faces harder than rock; they have refused to return" (Jeremiah 5:3).

Having a face that is "harder than rock" means a person refuses to receive correction. There is *no grief* in their heart for the things they do wrong. In fact, often there is *no recognition* in their heart that they have done anything wrong. This is a rebellious heart. A person with a *repentant heart* grieves over anything they do that violates God's ways.

Jeremiah went on to talk about the consequences of people who live in rebellion against God's ways, even though they know the truth. As a result of being disobedient and unrepentant, these people lost the protection of God on their lives.

Without repentance for our sin, it controls us. "Rebellion is as the sin of witchcraft, and stubbornness is as iniquity and idolatry" (1 Samuel 15:23). Only repentance will break the hold of sin on anyone's life. Without it, the death that comes along with sin that is not repented of fixes itself on our lives. Without repentance we are constantly paying the price for not living God's way.

God won't listen to our prayers when we live in rebellion. God doesn't hear our prayers when we have sin without repentance in our lives. "Your iniquities have separated you from your God; and your sins have hidden His face from you, so that *He will not hear*" (Isaiah 59:2, emphasis added). It can't get any clearer than that, but if you need something more to convince you, how about, "If I regard iniquity in my heart, *the Lord will not hear*" (Psalm 66:18, emphasis added). The psalmist who wrote that also said that when he cried out to God, He delivered him (verse 19), but it would not have happened if he had kept sin in his heart. When we want answers to our prayers, we must have clean hearts before God, and that takes a repentant heart.

A repentant heart is a humble heart. Pride destroys us. Humility brings us honor. "A man's pride will bring him low, but the humble in spirit will retain honor" (Proverbs 29:23). Pride is our downfall because it is the thing that will always keep us unrepentant. But a person with a humble heart can recognize his or her own sin. The opposite of humble is arrogant. Arrogance keeps us from seeing the truth about ourselves.

When our children were young, one of the ways Michael and I made sure that effective discipline was enacted when they did something wrong was to see if Christopher or Amanda had a repentant heart or not. In other words, were they really sorry for what they did or just sorry that they were caught? If it seemed as if the punishment didn't even faze them, then we had not done it right. We believed it was unfair to a child to not allow him or her to learn that there are consequences for doing wrong. When children don't learn that, they will grow up and find it *easy* to do wrong because they believe nothing will happen to them. When they have no discipline, they don't learn to discipline themselves. They don't learn self-control. How many times have we seen a vile murderer on trial who is declared guilty and yet has no remorse whatsoever? We see arrogance in him instead of humility. Surely that person never had serious enough consequences for his actions when he was growing up so that it formed in him a repentant heart.

I think looking for that repentant heart in each of our children made them receptive and responsive to being confronted and corrected as an adult when they got off the path. It didn't keep them from ever doing anything wrong, but it made them quick to repent.

We have all seen disastrous results when a young adult refused to receive correction from a parent or person in authority and rebelliously went on doing what they wanted to do. How many times have we observed young people reported on television as doing some horrendous thing, and we wonder, *How could they be so stupid? Don't they know they are throwing their lives away? Why did they think they could get away with it? What made them so arrogant as to belleve that there would be no consequences?*

Stephen, one of the men chosen to help the disciples after Jesus was crucified, was full of faith and the power of the Holy Spirit (Acts 6:5). He called the people questioning him "stiff-necked and uncircumcised in heart and ears." He said, "You always resist the Holy Spirit" (Acts 7:51). "Stiff-necked" means stubborn. "Uncircumcised heart" means unrepentant. By the very act of being stubborn and unrepentant, a person has resisted the Holy Spirit.

God will always bless a person who has a heart that is quick to hear from Him and repent when he has made mistakes. Pray that your adult children have hearts for God that are *compliant* and *repentant* toward Him. That means they are always *open to being corrected by the Holy Spirit.* We should also pray for repentant hearts for ourselves. It is what God wants for us all, and it will serve us well all the days of our lives.

Pray That They Desire to Know What God Has Done

God gives us a way to leave our children an inheritance that is *spiritual.* And this spiritual inheritance is more important than a monetary inheritance. With a spiritual inheritance, your adult children can start receiving it right away. So if you are not able to leave your adult children much in the way of an inheritance that can be deposited in a bank, don't worry because you can leave them a spiritual inheritance that will last their entire lifetime on earth. A spiritual inheritance is a legacy of good character, integrity, love, a good name, freedom from bondage, and blessings from God. In other words, your adult children will be more likely to inherit in themselves what they have seen modeled in you.

One of the ways you can share a spiritual legacy is to tell your children what God has done in your life. Asaph, a psalmist writing in the Old Testament, said of the things God had done, "I will open my mouth in a parable; I will utter dark sayings of old, which we have heard and known, and our fathers have told us. We will not hide them from their children, telling the generation to come the praises of the LORD, and His strength and His wonderful works that He has done" (Psalm 78:2–4). He went on to say that God commanded them to make these things known to their children so that future generations would know about them and not forget what the Lord had done. And that would help their adult children to put their hope in God, and it would keep them from becoming a stubborn and rebellious people who did not have right hearts or faithful spirits (Psalm 78:5–8).

There are those same words again: "stubborn and rebellious." What the psalmist is saying is that God wants parents to share with their children what He has done in their lives so their children won't become rebellious. We, too, need to make known to our children what God has done in *our* lives, so that they will not live in rebellion, and so they can teach these things to their own children. We want our adult children to never forget the goodness of God to us so that they will put their hope in the Lord and choose to live His way.

It says later in that psalm that the people who did *not* remember what God had done "tempted God, and limited the Holy One of Israel. *They did not remember His power: the day when He redeemed them from the enemy*" (Psalm 78:41–42, emphasis added). They ultimately ended up rebelling against God and turning to false gods (Psalm 78:56–58). That's why we have to share with our children all the times God has redeemed us from the hands of the enemy. We have to remember His power shown toward us in the past so that we will remember His power in the present when we need it most. And that will give us peace about the future.

It is important to communicate to your young children and your adult children what God means to you, how He has answered your prayers, and all the great things He has done for you in the past, plus what you anticipate He will do for you in the future. Tell them how you met the Lord, how He has changed you and provided for you, and how He is leading you today. It will strengthen *their* faith, as well as yours, because they will remember it, even many years later. Don't do it as if preaching a sermon. Simply find a good time to tell a story about the things God has done for you or taught you. When you are sharing this valuable part of your life with them, they will see how much it means to you and be impacted by it.

If you have only recently begun living God's way or have come to know the Lord since your children were grown, don't feel that it's too late to leave your adult children a spiritual inheritance. God will do great things for you now — even today. Ask Him to teach you something great from His Word. Ask the Holy Spirit to do something wonderful in your life right now. And when He does, write it down and remember to tell your adult children when the time is right. You can have a wealth of things to share about what God has done in a very short time.

You wouldn't be reading this book if you didn't want the best for your adult children and peace of mind for yourself. You want to help them in any way you can, but you don't want to take over God's place as the ultimate source for all their needs. You want to be able to influence and affect them in the godliest way, but you also want them to have their own strong relationship with God so that they will desire to live His way. You want them to love God the way you do.

The best way to help them learn to love God is to show them how much *God* loves *them.* And you do that by showing them how much *you* love them. Tell them of the good things you see *in* them and the great future you anticipate *for* them. Tell them what God's Word says about them. When your adult children see the love in you for them, they will open up and let you into their lives, and they will share their deepest concerns and needs. When they hear about God's love for them, they will open up to Him in a new and deeper way as well.

Lord, I pray for (name of adult child) and ask that You would give her (him) a heart to know You. I pray that just as it was said of Your good and faithful servant Daniel that "an excellent spirit was in him" (Daniel 6:3), may it also be said of my daughter (son) that an excellent spirit is in her (him). Draw her (him) close to You and enable her (him) to become more like You.

You have said in Your Word that You are the door by which anyone can enter and be saved (John 10:9). Keep her (him) from going through any other door except the path to eternity that You have for her (him). Where my daughter (son) has walked away from You in any way, cause her (him) to return to You with her (his) whole heart (Jeremiah 24:7). Enable her (him) to become a new creation in Christ as You have said in Your Word (2 Corinthians 5:17).

Give her (him) a heart of repentance — the kind of heart that is humble and turned toward You. Wherever there is any rebellion in her (him), I pray that You would create in her (him) a clean heart and renew a right spirit within her (him). Take away all pride that allows her (him) to think that she (he) can live without You. Give her (him) a desire to want what You want.

I pray that she (he) will love Your Word and will feed her (his) soul with it every day. Speak to her (his) heart and breathe life into every word so that it comes alive to her (him). Teach her (him) Your ways and Your laws and enable her (him) to do the right thing. I pray a silencing of the enemy's voice so that she (he) will hear Your Holy Spirit speaking to her (his) heart. Give her (him) a desire to live Your way. You have said in Your Word that when someone turns his ear away from hearing the law that even his prayer is an abomination (Proverbs 28:9). I pray that she (he) will never turn a deaf ear to Your laws.

God, help her (him) to have a passion for Your presence and Your Word. Help her (him) to sense the presence of Your Holy Spirit guiding her (him). I pray that she (he) will exalt You, love You enough to put You first, and serve You. May the outpouring of the Holy Spirit in her (his) life energize her (his) devotion to You. I pray that she (he) will draw life from her (his) relationship with You. Align her (his) will with Your will. Keep her (him) on your path so that she (he) is always where You want her (him) to be, doing what You want her (him) to do.

Help me to share with my adult daughter (son) all the good things You have done for me and my life. Make me more like You so that I can pass on to her (him) a rich spiritual inheritance. Enable me to inspire in her (him) a greater love for You because she (he) sees Your love in me.

In Jesus' name I pray.

Word Power

If you abide in Me, and My words abide in you, you will ask what you desire, and it shall be done for you. By this My Father is glorified, that you bear much fruit; so you will be My disciples.

John 15:7–8

In the way of righteousness is life, and in its pathway there is no death.

Proverbs 12:28

For the eyes of the LORD run to and fro throughout the whole earth, to show Himself strong on behalf of those whose heart is loyal to Him.

2 Chronicles 16:9

We know that God does not hear sinners; but if anyone is a worshiper of God and does His will, He hears him.

John 9:31

Draw near to God and He will draw near to you. Cleanse your hands, you sinners; and purify your hearts, you double-minded.

James 4:8

3

Pray That Your Adult Children Will Grow in Wisdom, Discernment, and Revelation

In order to have peace as parents, we have to pray for certain things to be true in the lives of our adult children. And then we have to trust God to answer those prayers. We can't be obsessing over everything that happens in their lives, because that would not only drive *us* crazy, but everyone around us as well. And that isn't the most effective way to pray for them anyway. We don't have to figure out every little detail; that's God's job. We have to pray for the big picture, pray for the most important issues, pray to neutralize the enemy's plans, pray about specifics if we know them, and pray for God's will to be done in each of our children's lives.

One of the most important issues we need to pray about for our adult children is that they function with godly wisdom, discernment, and revelation. These three gifts fro God alone can get them far in life and en able them to avoid potentially serious situations. How many of *us* — and how many of *them* — would have been spared some of the troubles we've had, if we'd only had those gifts fully functioning in our lives?

None of us can get through life successfully without wisdom, discernment, and revelation from God — especially not our adult children. The toxic society they have to wade through on a daily basis perpetuates so many lies and deceptions that only by having an understanding of the Word of God — as well as having a word *from* God in their hearts, given by the Spirit of wisdom — can they navigate around the pitfalls set as a trap for them to fall into. Only by having discernment and revelation from God can they walk successfully through the confusion and deception around them.

Having godly wisdom, discernment, and revelation can keep our adult children from being at the wrong place at the wrong time. It can prevent them from making bad decisions or choices. It can keep them from either trusting the wrong person or failing to trust the right one when they should. It can help them to choose a good thing over something that is not so good, especially hen the truth is not that easy to distinguish. It can enable them to foresee things they otherwise could not. It can give them a sense of danger or foreboding when it is in their best interest to have it. It can keep them out of trouble and away from harm.

Every one of us needs all three of these gifts from God functioning in our lives every day. We must ask God to make us wise and discerning, and we must ask Him to give us revelation about what we should do, where we should go, and how we should think. Not only can we pray for these things for ourselves, but we can pray for our adult children to have them as well.

Pray for Your Adult Child to Have Wisdom from God

So much is said about wisdom in the Bible that it is obvious we were not meant to live without it. But true wisdom comes only from God. It is not just information. We have more information than most of us really need and certainly more than is even safe in our world. Right now we collectively have enough information to blow the world apart if someone crazy, deluded, and evil enough gets themselves in the position to do it. What we need is more wisdom to handle the information we have.

Wisdom that is poured out by the Spirit of wisdom goes far beyond mere education and knowledge. It is a deep sense of the truth. We don't want our adult children to be the kind of people who are "always learning and never able to come to the knowledge of the truth" (2 Timothy 3:7). We want them to have godly wisdom, which is a *working knowledge* of the truth. When they have godly wisdom, they can make decisions quickly when they have to and those decisions will be right ones. They will be able to take the information they have and use it for good so that it bears fruit.

Our adult children are busy with their lives, trying to find out what works and what doesn't, who is good for their lives and who isn't. They are trying to figure out what they need to do to succeed and how hard they must work or study in order to accomplish that. They're thinking about establishing good relationships, finding the right marriage partner, or making their marriage work. They are trying to establish a solid home and raise a successful family. They are striving to find their place in the world, so they are busy testing what their limits and gifts are. They could figure all this out far better if they had wisdom from God. Having godly wisdom will make their lives go along far easier and smoother.

The Bible says that all we have to do is ask God for wisdom and He will give it to us. "If any of you lacks wisdom, let him ask of God, who gives to all liberally and without reproach, and it will be given to him" (James 1:5). We can ask for an outpouring of the Spirit of wisdom on behalf of our adult children as well. We must ask God to give them wisdom about how to think, act, and live.

When we have wisdom, we can see the consequences of our actions before we act, which enables us to make the right decision as to what action to take. Wisdom gives us deep understanding about the issues of our lives, and as a result it helps us to have the ability to reason. It gives us insight, good sense, and sound judgment. We can actually feel the Spirit of wisdom working in our lives. Have you ever made a decision about something you just *felt* was the right thing to do and later you found out that it was *precisely* the right thing to do — more than you even knew at the time? That is the Spirit of wisdom working in you, enabling you to make good decisions beyond what your natural capacity is to do so.

SEVEN EFFECTIVE WAYS TO PRAY FOR WISDOM

1. *Pray that your adult child will have the wisdom to fear God.* "The fear of the LORD is the beginning of wisdom" (Proverbs 9:10). All wisdom begins with a reverence for God and the ways of God. Having that kind of reverence makes room for the Spirit of wisdom to find a home in your adult child's heart.
2. *Pray that your adult child will have the wisdom to speak the right words to others.* "Do you see a man hasty in his words? There is more hope for a fool than for him" (Proverbs 29:20). Speaking the wrong words at the wrong time has gotten too many people into serious trouble. Knowing how to speak words that are right and timely can open doors of blessing and favor for them.
3. *Pray that your adult child will have the wisdom to not blaspheme the name of God.* "Remember this, that the enemy has reproached, O LORD, and that a foolish people has blasphemed Your name" (Psalm 74:18). Words that are not glorify-

ing to God are terribly destructive to the person using them. This is reflected in the third of the Ten Commandments that says anyone taking the Lord's name in vain will not be held guiltless by God (Exodus 20:7). If it sounds like blasphemy, those words carry consequences that are way too serious to risk.

4. *Pray that your adult child will be humble and not prideful.* "When pride comes, then comes shame; but with the humble is wisdom" (Proverbs 11:2). Having humility is always wise, but this implies that not only is it wise to be humble, but by being humble we grow in wisdom.
5. *Pray that your adult child will have the wisdom to not be drawn toward the wisdom of the world.* "Has not God made foolish the wisdom of this world?" (1 Corinthians 1:20). "For the wisdom of this world is foolishness with God" (1 Corinthians 3:19). What the world sees as wise is actually foolish in the eyes of God, and everything the world sees as foolish is wise in God's eyes.

For example, the world sees having faith in Jesus as foolish, but God sees it as the wisest thing we can do.

6. *Pray that your adult child will have the wisdom to love the Word of God.* "My son, if you receive my words, and treasure my commands within you, so that you incline your ear to wisdom . . . then you will understand the fear of the LORD, and find the knowledge of God" (Proverbs 2:1–2,5). Being open to God's Word and treasuring the laws and ways of God means that you are inclined toward the Spirit of wisdom, which enables you to discover and understand things you can't begin to understand without God's enablement.
7. *Pray that your adult child will have the wisdom to always seek the counsel of godly and wise people.* "Incline your ear and hear the words of the wise, and apply your heart to my knowledge" (Proverbs 22:17). "Blessed is the man who walks not in the counsel of the ungodly, nor stands in the path of sinners, nor sits in the seat of the scornful"

> (Psalm 1:1). It is important that the people who influence your adult children are godly people who spread wisdom in their direction. Pray that the only people who have your adult child's ear are people in whom dwells the Spirit of wisdom.

One long passage in the first chapter of Proverbs describes wisdom as a woman who calls out to us. "*Wisdom calls* aloud outside; she raises her voice in the open squares" (Proverbs 1:20, emphasis added). Below are highlights from that passage:

> How long, you simple ones, will you love simplicity? . . . Turn at my rebuke; surely *I will pour out my spirit on you;* I will make my words known to you (verses 22–23, emphasis added).
>
> *Because you disdained all my counsel,* and would have none of my rebuke, I also will laugh at your calamity (verses 25–26, emphasis added).
>
> *They will call on me, but I will not answer;* they will seek me diligently, but they will not find me. *Because they hated knowledge and did not choose the fear*

> *of the* L*ORD*, they would have none of my counsel (verses 28–30, emphasis added).
>
> Therefore *they shall eat the fruit of their own way . . .* For the turning away of the simple will slay them, and the complacency of fools will destroy them (verses 31–32, emphasis added).
>
> But *whoever listens to me will dwell safely,* and will be secure without fear of evil (verse 33, emphasis added).

In other words, the Spirit of wisdom wants to pour out wisdom upon us, but if we do not seek to have it and we refuse wise counsel, we will suffer the consequences. However, if we *seek* wisdom, we will live *safe* and *secure* lives.

Just as verse 23 above describes wisdom as *a spirit poured out on us,* the Bible also says that godly wisdom comes through the Holy Spirit of God. "To one is given the word of *wisdom* through the *Spirit,* to another the word of *knowledge* through the same *Spirit,* to another faith by the same Spirit, to another gifts of healings by the same Spirit, to another the working of miracles" (1 Corinthians 12:8–10, emnasis added).

In talking about the coming of the Lord Jesus many years before it happened, the prophet Isaiah said, "The Spirit of the LORD shall rest upon Him, the Spirit of *wisdom* and *understanding,* the Spirit of counsel and might, the Spirit of knowledge and of the fear of the LORD" (Isaiah 11:2, emphasis added).

The Bible says that Joshua "was *full of the spirit of wisdom,* for Moses had laid his hands on him" (Deuteronomy 34:9, emphasis added). We can lay our hands on our adult children and pray for them to be full of the Spirit of wisdom as well.

The essence of the Scriptures above is that God is ready to pour out the Spirit of wisdom upon anyone who desires to have it. Those who don't will experience calamity and destruction. Those who do want it will have it and, as a result, will dwell in safety and freedom from fear. The Spirit of wisdom poured out on your adult children will make their lives work far better. Mere education and worldly knowledge isn't enough. Wisdom that comes from God will help them take the information they have and use it to bear fruit in their lives. It will protect them. Pray for an outpouring of the Spirit of wisdom on your adult children so that they will know how to think, act, an live.

Pray for Your Adult Child to Have Godly Discernment

When your adult children have discernment, they will be able to understand what would normally be obscure to them. They will have insight into situations enabling them to see what most people cannot. For example, they will be able to discern the true character of a person, which can save them tremendous grief and trouble. How many people would have been spared terrible things if they would have only had discernment? How many young girls would not have been murdered or raped if they could have discerned the true character of the person they let into their lives who abused them?

Five Reasons Your Adult Children Need Godly Discernment

1. *When your adult children have discernment, they will always do the right thing.* Without it they can act foolishly. "Folly is joy to him who is destitute of discernment, but a man of understanding walks uprightly" (Proverbs 15:21). We don't want

our adult children to do anything foolish. We want them to have great understanding so they will walk the right way and do the right thing.

2. *When your adult children have discernment, they will be able to clearly see what is good and what is evil.* When God appeared to Solomon in a dream asking what he wanted the Lord to give him, Solomon replied, "Give to your servant an understanding heart to judge Your people, that I may discern between good and evil" (1 Kings 3:9). Solomon's answer pleased God because he did not ask for long life or riches or the lives of his enemies. Instead, he wanted the ability to clearly see what and who was good, and what and who was evil. God answered his request and gave him a wise and understanding heart.
3. *When your adult children have discernment, they will be able to see what is holy and clean and what is not.* "They shall teach My people *the difference between the holy and the unholy,* and cause them to discern between the unclean and the clean" (Ezekiel 44:23, emphasis

added). In this day of rampant enemy deception, we all need this gift from God in order to distinguish what is holy, clean, and good from that which is unholy, unclean, and evil. We and our adult children cannot always see the truth without it.

4. *When your adult children have discernment, they will be able to see what is right and what is wrong.* Paul prayed for the Philippians that they would discern what is best and live righteously. "This I pray, that your love may abound still more and more in knowledge and *all discernment,* that you may approve the things that are excellent, that you may be sincere and without offense till the day of Christ, being filled with the fruits of righteousness which are by Jesus Christ, to the glory and praise of God" (Philippians 1:9–11, emphasis added). Paul wanted people to be right before God. And that is what we want for ourselves and our adult children.
5. *When your adult children have discernment, they will be able to under-*

> *stand the things of God.* Paul said God reveals things to us by His Spirit. "We have received, not the spirit of the world, but the Spirit who is from God, that we might know the things that have been freely given to us by God" (1 Corinthians 2:12). He also said that "the natural man does not receive the things of the Spirit of God, for they are foolishness to him; nor can he know them, because they are spiritually discerned" (1 Corinthians 2:14). Many things can only be spiritually discerned by people who have the Holy Spirit dwelling in them and are therefore led by Him.

The good news is that discernment is something we can ask God for in prayer. "If you cry out for discernment, and lift up your voice for understanding, if you seek her as silver, and search for her as for hidden treasures; then you will understand the fear of the LORD, and find the knowledge of God" (Proverbs 2:3–5). If we fervently pray to God for discernment and understanding, He will give it to us, along with a deep *reverence for* and *knowledge of* Him.

We must pray that for our adult children a well.

Pray for Your Adult Child to Have Revelation from God

Having revelation means having knowledge given to you by God that you would not have had otherwise. He unveils what is already true but has been previously hidden to your mind and heart. In other words, it was true all along, but now God has revealed it to you so you can see it clearly. It is God who does the revealing rather than it being something *we* do to figure it out.

God reveals things to us in His Word as we read it, hear it, or speak it. We can read or hear a passage or verse of Scripture over and over and one day suddenly have new revelation about it that we have never seen before. God also reveals Himself to us as we walk with Him and communicate with Him in prayer so we can know Him better. God reveals things to us when we seek Him and His knowledge of a situation. "Lord, give me revelation about my future. Should I move to this town or another? Should I go to this church or that one? Should I be with this person or someone else?" When we keep asking Him for revelation, one day we will have it.

FOUR REASONS TO ASK GOD FOR REVELATION

1. *Revelation from God to our hearts gives us a vision for our lives.* This doesn't mean we know every detail, but we do know we have a future and that it is good. The Bible says, "Where there is no revelation, the people cast off restraint; but happy is he who keeps the law" (Proverbs 29:18). A person who doesn't have revelation from God cannot see the big picture and therefore nothing is holding him back from doing whatever he wants. He will be unrestrained because he has nothing guiding him and no regard for the future.
2. *Revelation from God means that He opens our eyes and gives us understanding and enlightenment about our purpose and calling.* And He reveals the greatness of His power on our behalf. The apostle Paul speaking to the Ephesians told them he prayed "that the God of our Lord Jesus Christ, the Father of glory, may give to you the spirit of wisdom and revelation in the knowl-

edge of Him, the eyes of your understanding being enlightened" so that they could know "what is the hope of His calling" and "what is the exceeding greatness of His power toward us who believe" (Ephesians 1:17–19). Who among us doesn't need that? That's why we must pray to have revelation for ourselves as well as for our adult children.

3. *Revelation from God helps us to make a right response — a response we would not have known to make without it — that will keep us from destroying ourselves.* "A man who wanders from the way of understanding will rest in the assembly of the dead" (Proverbs 21:16). Without revelation we can make disastrous decisions. Not only can our adult children not make right choices without revelation from God, they often cannot make *any* choices at all. All too common in our society today is the inability of young people to make life decisions — about anything! Often they have trouble deciding where to work, what to do, whom to marry, where

to go, and other important things in order to move their lives along. Only a word from God to their hearts can get them moving with any kind of certainty. Revelation changes everything. Without revelation from God, they don't know what to do and they can remain frozen in place.

4. *Revelation from God means that He reveals who He is to us.* When Jesus asked His disciples, "Who do you say that I am?" Peter answered, "You are the Christ, the Son of the living God." To which Jesus responded by saying Peter was blessed because "flesh and blood has not revealed this to you, but my Father who is in heaven" (Matthew 16:15–17). Peter knew who Jesus was because God had given him *revelation* about it. God will also give *us* revelation about Himself when we ask for it. We can pray for our adult children to have revelation from God about who He is as well.

Jesus said to His disciples that "no one knows who the Son is except the Father, and who the Father is except the Son, and the one to whom the Son wills to reveal Him" (Luke 10:22). Any revelation we get about who God is comes because Jesus wills to reveal Him.

So many people don't believe in God because they have never had a revelation as to who He is. When I received the Lord, I stepped out in faith and took a chance that He was real and that what the Bible said was true. But after that God revealed Himself to me when I was reading His Word, when I was hearing His Word taught, when I spent time in praise and worship, and while I was praying. I asked God for revelation about my life and about Him and He gave it to me. Little by little and step by step, that revelation of who God is gave me a vision for my life and a sense of purpose.

Pray for the heart of each of your adult children to desire godly wisdom, discernment, and revelation. These things are life-changing and will benefit them greatly every day of their lives.

PRAYER POWER

Lord, I pray that (name of adult child) will have wisdom that comes through Your Holy Spirit (1 Corinthians 12:8). Help him (her) to be strong, refusing to fall into the ways of the foolish. Help him (her) to have the wisdom to never blaspheme Your name. Bring strong conviction into his (her) heart whenever he (she) is tempted. Instead, I pray that he (she) will "let the high praises of God" be in his (her) mouth and "a two-edged sword" in his (her) hand (Psalm 149:6).

Lord, You have said that if we lack wisdom, we are to ask for it and You will give it to us (James 1:5). I come to You asking that You would pour out Your Spirit of wisdom upon my adult children. Give them wisdom to always speak the right word to others, to seek godly and wise counsel, to be humble and not prideful, and not be drawn toward the wisdom of the world.

Help him (her) to have the kind of sound wisdom that brings discretion, so that it will become life to his (her) soul (Proverbs 3:21–22). Give him (her) wisdom that will help him (her) always make good choices and decisions, and to trust the right people. Give him (her) wisdom that guides him (her) away from danger and protects him (her) from evil. Give him (her) a deep sense of the truth, and the ability to take information and make accurate judgments about it.

I know that Your Word is the two-edged sword You want in his (her) hand, so I pray that You would put a love in his (her) heart for the Scriptures and a desire to read the Bible every day. Engrave Your words on his (her) mind and heart so that they become life to him (her). Enable him (her) to retain Your words and keep your commands so he (she) can live (Proverbs 4:4).

Lord, You have said in Your Word that "a wise man will hear and increase learning, and a man of understanding will attain wise counsel" (Proverbs 1:5). I pray that my adult child will become filled with Your wisdom and be able to hear the truth and know it. Help him (her) to understand the fear of the Lord and have a heart of reverence for You. I pray that he (she) will "cry out for discernment" and lift up his (her) voice for understanding so that he (she) will "understand the fear of the LORD and find the knowledge of God" (Proverbs 2:3, 5). Give him (her) wisdom in all things so that he (she) will be shaped by Your hand and not the world.

I pray that You would give my adult child the ability to discern between good and evil, just as You gave that ability to Solomon. Help him (her) to discern between holy and unholy, clean and unclean, right and wrong. Give him (her) insight into people and situations, enabling him (her) to see what he (she) would otherwise not be able to see. Help him (her) to discern the true character of every person. Help him (her) to see the things that can only be spiritually discerned (1 Corinthians 2:14).

Lord, I pray that You would give my adult children revelation for their lives. Help them to be guided by that revelation in all they do. Don't let them become paralyzed with indecision because they don't have a word in their heart from You. Give them revelation that fills their minds and hearts with a vision for their lives that opens their eyes to what Your purpose and calling is for them. Give them the kind of revelation that enables them to make a right decision they would not have made without it. Most of all, I pray You would reveal who You are to them in such a way that they know it is a revelation from You.

In Jesus' name I pray.

Word Power

The fear of the LORD is the beginning of knowledge, but fools despise wisdom and instruction.
PROVERBS 1:7

The law of the wise is a fountain of life, to turn one away from the snares of death.
PROVERBS 13:14

The foolishness of a man twists his way, and his heart frets against the LORD.
PROVERBS 19:3

Whoever loves wisdom makes his father rejoice.
PROVERBS 29:3

A wise son heeds his father's instruction, but a scoffer does not listen to rebuke.
PROVERBS 13:1

4
Pray That Your Adult Children Will Find Freedom, Restoration, and Wholeness

God wants all of us to live in the freedom, restoration, and wholeness He has for us. No matter how well or how poorly we were raised, or how seemingly perfect or imperfect our life experiences have been, we all have things from which we need to be set free. Our adult children are no different. Even if they were raised in the best of homes by the greatest of parents, they will still need to move into freedom in Christ and become more like the Lord.

Each of our adult children are as susceptible as anyone to having wrong thoughts, negative emotions, sinful actions and attitudes, or things from the past affecting them adversely today, and they need freedom and liberty from the constraints of all that. They may experience oppression from the enemy of their soul trying to rob and destroy them, and so they must have the deliverance and restoration only God can bring. Regardless of what is happening their lives, they need to be transformed in the image of Christ. Without that, they cannot find the wholeness God has for them. The good news is that God is greater than anything our adult children may be shackled by, and His plans for each one of them include freedom from everything that separates them from all He has for their lives.

One of my favorite verses in the Bible says, "Now the LORD is the Spirit; and *where the Spirit of the Lord is, there is liberty* (2 Corinthians 3:17, emphasis added). This is an especially profound and life-changing Scripture, and it is so beautifully simple. It's saying that the Spirit of God *is* the Spirit of liberty. And when we are in the presence of God's Holy Spirit, we are set free from the things that bind us, blind us, hold us back, and keep us from becoming all we were created to be.

The key here is simply the presence of the Lord.

I don't mean that the presence of the Lord lacks complexity, for who can fully comprehend all He brings to our lives? But when we have a question about how we can find freedom and liberty, the answer is not complex. We simply have to be in His presence. True liberty does not happen apart from the Lord.

Transformation is found in the presence of God.

When we are in communion with the Spirit of God, we find freedom. That's why we must be in His presence as much as possible. And we need to pray for our adult children to have an understanding of — and a desire for — the presence of the Holy Spirit so they can find all the *freedom* and *liberty, deliverance* and *restoration, transformation* and *wholeness* God has for them.

Freedom and Liberty

In chapter 1 of this book, the very first prayer we prayed was to ask God to pour out His Spirit upon our adult children. When the Holy Spirit is poured out upon them, He brings many wonderful and vital gifts into their lives. One of those glorious aspects of the Holy Spirit that He brings with Him is the Spirit of liberty.

You may be thinking, *If we have already prayed for the Holy Spirit to be poured out on our adult children, why do we need to pray again for the Spirit of liberty to set them free?*

The answer to that is we have to pray specifically when there is a specific need. We are not only praying for our adult children to be open to all the Holy Spirit wants to do *in them,* we are also praying for the Holy Spirit to set them free from something in particular. The challenging part is that the Holy Spirit will not do what someone resists Him doing. He will pour out His Spirit on our lives, but He will not force His liberation upon us. He will not set us free if we don't want to be.

This is why praying for our adult children is so important. We can't force them to want to be free. And let's face it, there may be things we as parents want our adult children to be free of, but they don't see it the same way. They like their bad habit, bad influence, or bad choice. Our prayers for our adult children can help them recognize that they *do* need to be free and what they need to be free of, and our prayers can open their hearts up to want that freedom.

When they truly understand that the Holy Spirit is the Spirit of liberty and freedom, then they will seek after the presence of God and the flow of His Spirit in them. When they see it is by the power of His presence that the bonds of hell are broken, then they will strive to remove anything out of their lives that stands in the way of His power flowing through them.

Jesus went to the synagogue and read from the book of Isaiah saying, "The Spirit of the

LORD is upon Me, because He has anointed Me . . . *to proclaim liberty to the captives*" (Luke 4:18, emphasis added). He said other important things from that passage as well, but for the purpose of this chapter, let's concentrate on those six words that I italicized — *"to proclaim liberty to the captives."* After Jesus finished reading this passage He said, "Today this Scripture is fulfilled in your hearing" (verse 21).

This means *Jesus* is the fulfillment of that Scripture.

God has anointed *Jesus* to proclaim liberty to the captives.

The kind of freedom and liberty Jesus is talking about here means there is a release from anything other than the power of God over us. We are no longer hampered or restricted from whatever God wants to do in our lives. When we receive the Lord, we are immediately set free from slavery to sin. We become slaves of righteousness instead (Romans 6:18). And we can be liberated from anything that tries to keep us from doing that.

Your adult child may know the Lord and His laws and yet still be taken captive in some way by someone or some influence. If you are aware of anything specific your adult child needs to be set free of — a wrong mind-set or attitude, a bad habit, an ungodly person, an unhealthy influence — pray for her (him) to find the freedom God has for her (him). If you are not sure what she (he) needs to be free of, ask God to reveal whatever must be seen so you can pray accordingly.

Often parents are the last to know about the things their adult children need to be set free from because parents are the ones from whom adult children try the hardest to hide these things. We can never assume we know everything there is to know about our adult children. Only God knows that. But He will give us revelation when we ask Him for it. And He will show us how to pray.

One of the greatest things we can do for our adult children is to get free ourselves. This is part of that spiritual heritage we leave to them. I have lived long enough to see both the children of the righteous and the children of the unrighteous grow up from infancy to become adults. I have seen distinct blessings on the children of believers who lived God's way that I have not seen in the children of the unbelievers. There is something of character, depth, protection, richness of soul, fulfillment, and a sense of life working out that happens in the children of the righteous. Notice I didn't say the children of the perfect. Or the children of parents who never made mistakes. Or the children of parents who had it all figured out from the beginning. I said the children of the righteous. Your righteousness comes because of Jesus in you. "Jesus in you" can begin at anytime He is invited into your heart — or anytime you return to Him after you have fallen away.

The blessings of a righteous life — a life lived God's way — can flow to your adult children today. And even more so when you get free of anything that hinders the flow of the Holy Spirit in *you.* Whatever you can get free of will affect your adult children's lives. Even though they may not be set free at the same time you are, your freedom will make it easier for them to find freedom themselves because they see it can be done and that gives them faith to believe that it's possible. Also, whenever you are set free of anything, something is broken in the spirit realm, and that can carry over and manifest in a powerful way in the physical realm. For example, a parent being set free from alcoholism by the power of the Holy Spirit will have a great impact on the ability of an adult child struggling to get free from the same thing.

The first of the Ten Commandments says,

"You shall have no other gods before Me." The second commandment says, "You shall not make for yourself a carved image . . . you shall not bow down to them nor serve them. For I, the LORD your God, am a jealous God, *visiting the iniquity of the fathers upon the children to the third and fourth generations of those who hate Me, but showing mercy to thousands, to those who love Me and keep My commandments*" (Exodus 20:3–6, emphasis added).

You may be thinking as I did when I first read that commandment, *This is not about me. I have never carved a golden calf and I don't bow down to any man-made image.* But the truth is that there are many ways we can have an image in our minds about what we want that we bow down to in our hearts. We carve golden ideas about what we think we need to have, or should be, or want to accomplish — or what our children need to have or be or accomplish — and we lift those images high in our hearts every day, even above the will of God. When what *we* want becomes more important than what *God* wants, it is an idol in our hearts. Any one of us can easily fall into that kind of hidden sin.

God says in this second commandment that the consequences of the sins of the parents will be visited upon the children, grandchildren, and great-grandchildren of those who do not love the Lord and live His way. Of course, all it would take is someone in one of those generations to say, "As for me and my house, we will serve the Lord, and so I pray in the name of Jesus that this sin and its consequences stop here and now," and that generational curse would be broken.

Ask God to show you any place in your life where you are continually paying the consequences for something that needs to be broken. Ask Him to open your eyes to whatever you are living with that you should not be. Ask Him to convict you of any way in which you are not walking in obedience to His will and His laws. Ask Him to reveal anything you are worshipping other than Him. When we are cleansed from the vestiges of all sin, we do not pass any propensity for it down to our children.

I ask you, in the light of that Scripture above about God visiting the *iniquities* of the fathers upon their offspring, is it not safe to believe that He will also visit the *blessings* that come as a result of a parent's *righteousness* upon their offspring? In other words, if we pass down consequences for the things we do wrong, doesn't it stand to reason that we will pass down the rewards for the things we do right? That's what the words mean in the last part of this second commandment that talk about God *"showing mercy to thousands, to those who love Me and keep My commandments."*

The good news is that it is never too late to start loving God and living His way so you can reap the benefits of His mercy. No matter what has happened, or *is* happening, with your adult child, it is not too late for the liberation, healing, and redemption of the Lord to change things in a miraculous way. And it can start with you.

You don't want to pass on to your adult children memories of a loveless, lifeless, powerless, passionless spirituality. You want to exhibit to them a loving, dynamic, powerful, passionate, exciting, hope-filled, compelling, living relationship with the Lord. You want your adult children to know the Lord as the Almighty God for whom nothing is impossible. It's worth praying that God will reveal to you — as well as to your adult children — anything you need to be set free from, and then ask the Holy Spirit to overflow you *all* with His liberating presence.

Knowing the truth can liberate us. Jesus said, "If you abide in My word, you are My disciples indeed. *And you shall know the truth, and the truth shall make you free*" (John 8:31–32, emphasis added). He was talking about *God's* truth here. We can be set free from something every time we read the Bible and the Holy Spirit brings it alive to our hearts. Pray your adult children will know the truth that sets them free.

Sometimes, however, we are shackled by something and we need the Deliverer — Jesus — to deliver us from its clutches. Deliverance means getting free of anything that holds us captive other than God. It means being rescued from someone or something that separates us from the Lord. Jesus delivered us from sin, death, and hell, so when we receive Him, we receive that deliverance. But through our own sinful thoughts and carelessness we can work ourselves into bondage to sin once again and need to be delivered from it.

One of the things Jesus also said when He spoke of how the Spirit of the Lord was upon Him was that God had anointed Him *"to set at liberty those who are oppressed"* (Luke 4:18, emphasis added). Apparently, it is one thing to be *captive* and another to be *oppressed.* He *proclaimed* liberty to the captives, but He *set at liberty* those who were oppressed. Sometimes we are liberated just because He said so; other times we give place to sin in our lives and become oppressed by the enemy, so we need the Deliverer to set us free.

Jesus went on to say that "whoever commits sin is a slave of sin," but "if the Son makes you free, you shall be free indeed" (John 8:34–35). James, the brother of Jesus, said, "You do not have because you do not ask" (James 4:2). We need to ask for deliverance, for ourselves and our adult children, so Jesus can set us completely free.

When we ask God for deliverance, not only will He deliver *us,* but He will also set our adult children free from whatever is binding them or keeping them from becoming all God made them to be. But they have to want to be set free. They have to want to be rid of all sin. If you have an adult child who does not want to be free from something that you would like her (him) to be free of, pray for her (his) eyes be opened to the need for deliverance from whatever has bound her (him). Pray that she (he) will want freedom *from* it more than bondage *to* it.

Sometimes we need deliverance, even

though we've done nothing wrong. After Jesus was crucified and resurrected from the dead, King Herod persecuted the believers — the church. He killed James, the first of the 12 apostles to be martyred. Then he arrested Peter with the intention of killing him too, as soon as the Passover ended. In prison, Peter was chained between two soldiers and surrounded by 16 soldiers in all. But there was constant prayer going up for Peter by the believers at the time. While he was sleeping, an angel of the Lord stood by him and a bright light shone into the prison. The angel told Peter to get up, and when he did, the chains fell off of his hands. The angel then instructed him to put on his clothes and sandals and follow him (Acts 12:1–8).

As Peter and the angel walked past the guards, no one saw them. And when they came to the big iron gate that kept them locked inside, it opened by itself (verse 10). As soon as Peter was free, the angel disappeared and Peter realized that God had *completely delivered* him from the hands of the enemy.

Herod symbolizes Satan with his never-ending attack on believers. Peter is the believer who had been put into chains, even though he had done nothing wrong. Satan's plan was to destroy Peter, so Peter needed a miracle of deliverance. And God delivered him from an impossible situation in response to the fervent prayer of others. Once liberated, Peter went to where the people were still praying and told them how God had set him free from the hands of the enemy. The unceasing prayers of the believers brought deliverance and freedom for Peter.

I go to a church that is very evangelistic. We plant churches in the United States and all over the world — especially in places where it is extremely dangerous to be a Christian. I cannot mention names of people or even the countries I am talking about because of the danger it would be to the pastors and their families. One particular pastor, whom I will call William, started a Christian church in one of the most dangerous countries for a Christian. That church grew and was thriving covertly, but William was eventually arrested for talking to someone about Jesus. The punishment for such a thing in that country is death. He went to trial with no legal representation and no jury — only a judge to decide his fate. He was, of course, declared guilty and sentenced to death.

Our church prayed fervently for William

and his family, and so did our sister churches worldwide. We prayed in groups, in special prayer meetings, and also alone in our own prayer closets. When we heard William had been sentenced to death, we continued to pray passionately for his release, all the while preparing ourselves for the worst. But one day news came to us that the decision of the judge who had heard William's case and pronounced the death sentence upon him was suddenly replaced by a decision of another judge. This second judge, for reasons unknown to us, reversed the previous judge's ruling and let William go. We were all amazed at what God did. The situation was *absolutely impossible,* yet the God of the impossible did an *absolute miracle.*

If God can do the kinds of miracles He did for Peter and William in response to the prayers of believers, how hard would it be for Him to set your adult child free from whatever imprisonment or sentence that has been pronounced upon his or her life? I tell you nothing is impossible for God when it comes to your adult children.

If your adult child has been imprisoned by the enemy, or the enemy is trying to encroach upon your adult child's life, you need reinforcements in prayer. Don't hesitate to ask others to pray with you. Constant, unceasing, unrelenting prayer is the key to freedom and deliverance for yourself and your adult children. God can turn a battle any way He wants it to go in response to prayer — especially when two or more are praying together.

No two people could have been more hopelessly imprisoned, or closer to execution with no possibility of a reprieve, than Peter or William. Yet they were both set free by the power of the Holy Spirit in response to unceasing prayer of the believers. At the same time people were praying for Peter, God shone His light into the prison so he could see. Pray that God will shine a light into any prison where your adult children are locked up so that they can see clearly and follow the Holy Spirit to freedom.

Along with deliverance, God will bring restoration *of all that went missing from our lives because we were in bondage to something.* That means He will restore the years that the locusts have eaten. And this is great news to any person whose life has in some way been devoured by the enemy. Whatever you have seen eaten away from your life or the lives of your adult children — the lost years, lost opportunities, lost relationships, lost health, lost abilities, lost freedom —

you can ask God to bring restoration and He will.

Restoration doesn't mean that if your adult child has had ten years of trouble since the time he was 20, that now God will suddenly make him 20 again. But it does mean that the God who delivered him out of trouble will bring a future with new opportunities, new health, new relationships, new abilities, and new freedom in Christ.

The Bible says that "the posterity of the righteous will be delivered" (Proverbs 11:21). That means our adult children will be set free. But they have to turn back to the Lord. "Turn us back to You, O LORD, and we will be restored; renew our days as of old" (Lamentations 5:21). Pray for your adult children to always be turned toward the Lord so they can find restoration.

The confidence we have in approaching God is "that if we ask anything according to His will, He hears us. And if we know that He hears us" — whatever we have asked — then we know that we will have what we asked of Him (1 John 5:14–15). The key is asking according to His will. We need revelation from God and His Word to know His will when we pray. We can ask for that too.

Transformation and Wholeness

Life doesn't work when something is broken. That's why God takes broken people — broken hearts, broken minds, broken spirits — and makes them whole. He takes the broken pieces of our lives and not only puts them back together again, but He also makes something beautiful and good out of those pieces. In order for that kind of wholeness to happen, we must be liberated from anything that limits the transformation God wants to do in our lives.

Wholeness for our adult children means, among other things, having a healthy sense of who they are in the Lord, who God made them to be, and what the gifts are that God put in them. It entails getting free of whatever is hindering that revelation. It means separating themselves from anything that separates them from God. It means spending time in God's presence where wholeness is found.

Even growing up in the best of Christian homes, it's hard for children to get through their childhood and teenage years without some kind of brokenness. Something someone said or did, or didn't do or say, or something they saw or experienced, can trouble their young minds and break their hearts. Broken relationships without healing and restoration can affect all of their relationships, and especially their relationship with God. If any of your adult children have seen heartbreaking things in their lives, you can pray for them to be set free from all bad memories.

I have known many adult children who were broken people and their lives had broken down, but through the prayers of their parents they were set free and their lives were put back together. God acted powerfully in response to prayer. That is not to say that a person who doesn't have a parent praying for them cannot get free. If that were true, I would not be here today. I grew up in a house with a severely mentally ill mother who was physically and verbally abusive. I tried everything to get free of the pain of my childhood, but it only brought me deeper into depression, anger, fear, and hopelessness. Every day I could feel my life sinking down into a deep, dark hole from which I feared I might never escape. It was the prayers of others that saved my life and brought me to the Lord. And through the prayers of others, He lifted me out of that pit; set me free from depression, fear, and anxiety; completely transformed my life; and made me whole. I lost too many years living the wrong way, but God has restored those years beyond what I dreamed possible. If He can do that for me, imagine how much He can do for someone who has the fervent prayers of a parent behind him (her).

Every step we take toward renewing our minds and souls in the Lord transforms us more and more into the image of Christ. Granted, we all have a long way to go, but each moment of transformation brings us closer to the wholeness God has for us.

Do you see what all this means to you and your adult children? It means that no matter what it is they need to be set free from, your prayers can be instrumental in that happening. Of course, there are things your adult children have to do for themselves. Just as Peter had to clothe himself before he was let out of prison, your adult children will have to clothe themselves too. Pray that they will put on the garments of righteousness, praise, humility, and faith. And know that God will honor *your* righteousness, praise, humility, and faith in prayer until *theirs* kicks in.

Lord, I pray that my adult children will find all the freedom and liberty You have for them. Set them free from anything that separates them from You. I pray for an outpouring of Your Holy Spirit of liberty upon them so that great breakthrough can come in any area of their lives where it is needed. Whether they have been imprisoned by their own sins, or the lies and plans of the enemy have held them captive, I pray You would liberate them. If they need to be set free from a wrong mind-set or an ungodly belief, help them to move into freedom in Christ.

I don't know all the ways my adult children need to be set free, but You do, Lord. Shed Your light on whatever must be illuminated. Reveal anything that is holding them back. Show me how to pray so they can be liberated from everything that keeps them from all You have for them.

Lord, I know You are greater than anything my adult children may be shackled by, and Your plans for their lives are for total freedom. Holy Spirit, help them to understand that where You are, there is liberty (2 Corinthians 3:17). Help them to find the transformation that can only be found in Your presence.

Teach my daughter (son) to seek Your presence in the *Word,* in *prayer,* and in *praise* and *worship.* Help her (him) to know the truth in Your Word that sets her (him) free. Help her (him) to see the truth about any sin in her (his) life. Where the enemy is oppressing her (him), remove the blinders from her (his) eyes so she (he) can recognize the truth about that too. Where a cruel sentence has been handed down upon her (his) life, bring a miraculous reprieve and give her (him) the ability to recognize that it is You who has liberated her (him).

Jesus, Your Word says that You came "to proclaim liberty to the captives" and "to set at liberty those who are oppressed" (Luke 4:18). I pray that wherever my adult child has been held captive by anything, You would set her (him) free. Where she (he) is being oppressed by the enemy, I pray that You would deliver her (him) from that torment. Break any stronghold that the enemy has erected against her (him).

Lord, I know that one of the greatest things I can do for my adult children is to get free myself. Show me where I have allowed myself to become tied up in any way — either by my own thoughts and actions or by the enemy of my soul. Show me if I am entertaining anything in my mind, my heart, or my life that is not of You so I can be free of it. Deliver me from everything that hinders the flow of Your Spirit in me. I pray that my freedom will be apparent to my adult children and that it will inspire a desire for freedom in them. Help me to have the kind of dynamic, powerful, and hope-filled relationship with You that instills in them a quest for the same. Enable me to always live Your way so that both my adult children and I will reap the benefits of Your mercy (Exodus 20:6). May the blessings of my life, lived according to Your laws, flow to them.

I pray You would make whole anything in my adult child's life that is broken. Bring restoration of all that has been lost. Restore lost time, lost opportunities, lost health, lost relationships, or whatever else that has been taken from her (him). Where there has been valuable time wasted, restore the years the locusts have eaten (Joel 2:25). Bring the transformation needed so that she (he) can receive the wholeness You have for her (him).

Once she (he) has been set free, help her (him) to stay free. Keep her (him) from becoming entangled again. I say to my daughter (son) by the power of Your Spirit, "Stand fast therefore in the liberty by which

Christ has made us free, and do not be entangled again with a yoke of bondage" (Galatians 5:1). I say to You, Lord, "Be exalted, O God, above the heavens, and Your glory above all the earth; that Your beloved may be delivered" (Psalm 108:5–6).

In Jesus' name I pray.

Word Power

Because he has set his love upon Me, therefore I will deliver him . . . He shall call upon Me, and I will answer him; I will be with him in trouble; I will deliver him and honor him. With long life I will satisfy him.
Psalm 91:14–16

The Lord gives freedom to the prisoners.
Psalm 146:7

The angel of the Lord encamps all around those who fear Him, and delivers them.
Psalm 34:7

The horse is prepared for the day of battle, but deliverance is of the Lord.
Proverbs 21:31

He who trusts in his own heart is a fool, but whoever walks wisely will be delivered.
Proverbs 28:26

5
Pray That Your Adult Children Will Understand God's Purpose for Their Lives

One rapidly spreading epidemic I see today among many adult children is confusion about what their purpose is in life. One of the things contributing to such confusion is that they are getting far more input from the world than they are from God. The ways of the world are often confusing, while God's ways are clear. And when life is lived *His* way, it brings greater clarity.

Simply reading God's Word, for example, can dissolve confusion. But many adult children spend far too much of their spare time watching television, looking at their computers, or engaged in other forms of entertainment, and far too little time, if any, reading the Bible. And anyone receiving more input from the media than they are from God can wind up wandering without a sense of purpose. When God's voice is drowned out, there is no true guide and they can easily be headed in the wrong direction.

Having a sense of purpose in life doesn't necessarily mean your adult children know every detail about what they should do and where they should go, but they will have an inkling regarding some particulars. They may not know *exactly* what they want to do in life, but they will know, for example, that they want to go to college or to a trade school to become educated and skilled at a profession. Some adult children without a sense of purpose don't even have a leading in their hearts about that. Without any leading from God, they can become aimless, or they may pursue something that will ultimately be wrong for them and end up wasting precious years of their lives before they figure it out. Without a leading from God about what to do, they can become afraid to step out and do anything at all because they fear they might fail. But when they have that leading from God, even though they may have thoughts of possible failure, it doesn't stop them from moving ahead with what God is calling them to do.

Middle school and high school experiences can do a great deal to harm a teenager's sense of purpose. If they are made fun of or humiliated for any reason, it destroys their sense of who they are. If they feel unacceptable in comparison to others, they may have a harder time discovering and learning to value their unique talents and gifts. When every day is an endurance test and they are just trying to survive, they can fail to establish a sense of purpose.

My daughter, Amanda, spent so much time in high school berating herself because she was dyslexic. I say *was* because she has overcome that so miraculously that one would never know she ever struggled with it. But it took some serious steps and much fervent prayer.

For years she had asked me to homeschool her, and I was reluctant because I knew she was intelligent and gifted and I believed she needed the socialization of attending school with others. But I was wrong. School almost destroyed her. At the end of her sophomore year in high school, she again *begged* me to homeschool her. I could see the tremendous hurt that had accumulated in her heart over years of what she felt was failure and humiliation.

I knew she would work hard because she had always worked harder in school than most of her peers and for so little reward. I also recognized that she had completely lost the joy of learning she'd had in abundance as a child. I had to take on the challenge, even though I doubted my ability to do it well. I knew I could teach her classes like history, geology, geography, science, English literature, composition, and Bible, because those were the classes I loved. But I worried about math. I had always done well in math in school, but that was then. The new math was beyond my ability to catch up on with such short notice. So my husband and daughter and I prayed, and God answered our prayers for a wonderful and godly tutor.

Homeschool was the perfect thing for Amanda, and we had so much fun doing it. History came alive for both of us, and we went on wonderful field trips to see historical places. English became a joy as she read for fun and wrote amazing research papers and essays. We studied the Bible together every day and prayed about her purpose and future. I began to see her joy of learning blossom once again.

After high school she went to a local college in the music and entertainment department, but she didn't like being constantly judged for her looks and talent on top of her own unrelenting self-judgment. She had been a great singer from the time she was small. She won an all-school talent contest, had one of the leads in a dramatic musical in the city, sang professionally for a while doing background vocals for other artists, and recorded an album with two other singers. Michael and I had always encouraged her in that direction because we thought that this gift was obviously what she was created to do. But she didn't like the pressure and competition, nor the constant scrutiny and judgment that a career in music demanded. She wanted a simple and peaceful life, and the music industry — even the Christian music industry — was anything but simple. She didn't have the heart for it. The bottom line was that she had no sense of purpose with regard to music.

Amanda had several different part-time jobs, from store clerk to waitressing, and each one was a great experience because she learned to deeply respect the people who work hard at those kinds of jobs full-time to support their families. Still, she did not have a clear vision for her life, except that she came to the conclusion that those jobs were only a means to an end but not her ultimate purpose. So we were progressing.

One day as Amanda and I were praying together specifically for God to open up her eyes to what His purpose was for her, it suddenly came to her what she should do with her life. She knew she was meant to help people by means of physical therapy. I had mentioned that to her earlier when I was telling her about the gifts I had observed in her. She'd always had remarkable healing hands. Being raised around physical therapists — because I have always needed so much of it due to injuries I've had — had given her a natural sense of how to relieve someone's pain. And she believed in the therapeutic and healing powers of it. She immediately knew that was it.

Amanda enrolled in a school for that specialty and totally found her niche. She loved the instructors, found great rapport with other students, and is now devoted to practicing different kinds of physical therapy that can encourage healing in the body. Everything fell into place and doors opened up for her one after another. She says her new life verse is: "Let nothing be done through selfish ambition or conceit, but in lowliness of mind let each esteem others better than himself. Let each of you look out not only for his own interests, but also for the interests of others" (Philippians 2:3–4). Amanda feels she is 100 percent where she is supposed to be and she is doing what God created her to do — to give health and life to people who are hurting. What changed was her sense of purpose.

It is extremely satisfying as a parent to see your adult child have a clear sense of purpose in his or her life.

If Your Adult Child Lacks a Sense of Purpose

Your adult child may have had a sense of purpose from the time he (she) stood up in his (her) crib. Or you may have a 30-year-old lying around your house because he (she) has moved back in for the fifth time after another job didn't pan out. Or perhaps he (she) never moved out in the first place, at which point I would suggest getting yourself a pair of knee pads because you are going to need to involve yourself in some fervent intercession. In fact, I would say to take a day every month to fast and pray about that adult child. Ask God to break down any barriers keeping him (her) from receiving a vision for his (her) life and a sense of God's purpose and calling.

Allow me to suggest that an adult child who continues on with no sense of purpose is a dangerous thing. I guarantee that kids who commit suicide, take drugs, drink habitually, commit crimes, or go on murderous rampages have no sense of purpose. If they did, they would not do anything to violate that purpose. They would not want to get off the path God has for them. But those are extreme examples.

If your adult child doesn't seem to have a sense of purpose right now, don't be worried by it. Instead, trust God to give that to him (her) because you are praying for it. But if it doesn't happen right away, don't stop praying. I know wonderful godly parents whose son didn't seem to have any sense of purpose at all. He was a believer, raised in a dynamic Christian church, and had godly friends all around him. I have known this family from the time their son was about six years old, and he could not have had a more wonderful home and upbringing. After high school he didn't want to go to college or do much of anything else. His parents prayed and prayed for him to have a sense of the calling God had on his life. A couple of years out of high school he was still not working or getting any further education, but then he went on a mission trip with his church and the Holy Spirit broke through.

He came home from that trip with a vision for his life to help others. He went to college, got a bachelor's degree and then a master's degree, and then he met a wonderful girl and got married. He has now completed a doctoral program. All this happened because he got a vision for his life and a strong sense of purpose from God.

Some kids take longer than others to find their niche. That is not necessarily a bad thing or a reflection on the parents or the adult child. Everyone has their own path and their own timetable. Don't beat yourself up if you see your adult child struggling to find his (her) place in the world. And don't berate him (her) verbally, because it will only alienate him (her) from you and won't accomplish anything. You can pray, strongly encourage, and get him (her) to talk about himself (herself) and the dreams, hopes, ideas, likes, and dislikes he (she) has. Tell him (her) how much you love and admire him (her). Tell him (her) of the good traits and gifts *you* see in him (her).

Ask God to reveal what you need to see about your unmotivated adult children. Try to steer them away from sitting in their rooms all day listening to music or surfing the Internet. This will not help them discover their purpose. It will instead put them into a brain fog. If they are going to live in your house, make them part of your household. Give them chores to do and have expectations of what they are to contribute, just as you or your spouse or whoever else lives there is expected to do. Require them to live by your rules. Having low expectations for adult children doesn't do them any good, just as having expectations that are too high doesn't either.

Michael and I let our adult children live in our house until they were financially ready to move out into good, safe places when they were in their twenties. They had lived away from home in college in apartments off campus with roommates. Once they were out of college, they each worked full-time and saved money for a down payment on their own condominium, which they each bought when they were financially ready to take on the responsibility.

I can see why parents allow their adult children to live with them so long when they are not working. It's cheaper, and at least you know they are safe. But there comes a point where a line must be drawn. For example, saying, "Yes, you can stay here, but you have to either be working or going to school or both. You can't be doing nothing." An adult child will not find his (her) purpose lying in front of the TV or a video game. He (she) will not find it sleeping all day and staying out all night with his (her) friends. He (she) may not find it working in a fast-food restaurant either, but at least while he (she) is working there he (she) may realize what his (her) purpose *isn't.* And that will help in the process of elimination.

However, your adult children cannot live with you forever even under these circumstances, for then they will never discover what God has for them. Unless they are handicapped and need your full-time care, at some point they must start living the lives God has called them to. You and they will not be happy until they do. Pray for your adult children to have a sense of purpose from God, because it will propel them to do whatever they need to do in order to fulfill that. An adult child with no sense of purpose will do nothing, but an adult child *with* a sense of purpose will do what it takes to get where they need to be.

If Your Adult Child Needs Direction

Every adult child needs a sense of direction. Should they go away to school or stay close to home? Should they find work in another city or in their hometown? Should they work with this company or that one? Even if they don't know their purpose, they need to take steps in some direction. And you want it to be the right one.

After the fall of Jerusalem, the people who were left there asked Jeremiah to pray for them to have direction from the Lord so they would know what to do — whether to stay where they were or go to Egypt. Jeremiah prayed, but the answer did not come right away. "*And it happened after ten days* that the word of the LORD came to Jeremiah" (Jeremiah 42:7, emphasis added). Jeremiah had a direct line to God and he had God's favor, yet he still had to wait for the answer. Always keep in mind that you, too, have a direct line to God. He's called Jesus. And you have favor with God because of Jesus living in you. And you can pray for direction for your adult child by the power of the Holy Spirit. But don't get discouraged if the answer doesn't come right away. It may come suddenly, like a light switch being turned on. Or it may come gradually, like a sunrise. No matter how the answer comes, it will be right on target because it is from the Lord.

The problem with the Israelites was that they had already made up their minds *before* they asked Jeremiah to ask God for them. It didn't matter that God instructed them to stay in Jerusalem; they were determined to go to Egypt anyway. Because they didn't listen to God's direction, they were destroyed. Pray for your adult children not only to hear God's direction, but to do what He says.

It is said of Jerusalem that the city fell because she did not consider her destiny. "She did not consider her destiny; therefore her collapse was awesome; she had no comforter" (Lamentations 1:9). The reason this happened was not because God had no mercy on the people; it was because they had turned away from God and pursued idols and were entirely unrepentant. The people didn't take into consideration that their sin would lead to destruction. They did what they wanted, thinking there would be no consequences. This is exactly what happens when people try to live without a God-given sense of destiny. Pray that your adult children will be wise enough to consider their destiny. In order to do so, they will need to consult with God so He can keep them headed in the right direction.

Our adult children can have a sense of direction and yet still have difficulty making decisions. When they can't make decisions and choices about important things, we need to pray for an outpouring of the Holy Spirit upon them to help them figure things out. And we have to *keep* praying until they have their answers.

If Your Adult Child Already Has a Sense of Purpose

Consider yourself blessed if your adult child already has a sense of purpose. All you have to do is pray that they don't lose sight of what that is, and that God will continue to help them define it and enable them to take the right steps in order to see that purpose realized in their life.

Keep in mind, however, that it is always possible for anyone to lose their sense of purpose by becoming overworked, overwhelmed, stressed, sick, disappointed, doubtful, or by making a wrong decision, experiencing repeated failure, listening to a bad influence, or becoming confused by the enemy. If ever you see that happening in your adult children, pray for them to hear afresh from the Holy Spirit and get back on track.

The apostle Paul told the Ephesians he prayed that the eyes of their understanding would be enlightened, so that they could know what the hope of His calling was (Ephesians 1:18). You can pray the same thing for your adult children. Pray that their eyes will be opened to see what God's calling is on their lives. Pray that they will understand that their purpose and calling will be realized as their relationship with the Lord deepens.

Lord, I pray for (name of adult child) to have a sense of purpose for his (her) life and the ability to understand that purpose with clarity. Give him (her) the Spirit of wisdom and revelation so that the eyes of his (her) understanding will be enlightened. Help him (her) to know what is the hope of Your calling and what is the exceeding greatness of Your power on his (her) behalf (Ephesians 1:17–19). I pray that Your plans to fulfill the destiny and purpose You have for him (her) will succeed, and not the plans of the enemy.

Enable him (her) to separate himself (herself) from all the distractions of this world and turn to You in order to hear Your voice. Keep him (her) from wasting his (her) life pursuing anything that takes him (her) off the path You have for him (her). I pray that every experience will lead him (her) closer to You and further from anything that undermines Your plans for him (her). I pray that all he (she) does will support that purpose and not postpone the realization of it. Enable him (her) to always be growing in his (her) relationship with You.

Lord, show me how to pray specifically for my adult child's purpose, direction, and calling. Give me insight and revelation. Help me to encourage him (her) and give helpful input without being judgmental or overbearing. Where boundaries need to be drawn, show me clearly what they should be and help me to establish them. Where the answer seems to be a long time in coming, help me to not lose heart. Keep me strong in prayer until Your purpose is fulfilled.

Help my adult children to hear Your voice so they have a word in their heart from You. Let it become a springboard propelling them in the right direction. Give them a strong sense of direction and purpose that transcends all fear, hesitation, laziness, defeat, and failure.

When my adult children *do* have a sense of purpose, I pray that they will not lose it. Give them the wisdom and motivation to take the right steps every day. Enable them to understand what is most important in life, so they can make decisions and choices easily. I pray they will never fail to consider their destiny in every choice they make and in everything they do. Help them to not have their minds made up without consulting You. Keep them from insisting on what *they* want instead of wanting what *You* want.

Instill in my adult children a desire to always be in the center of Your will. To them

I say, "May God give you the desires of your heart that are in His will, and fulfill all your purpose" (Psalm 20:4).

In Jesus' name I pray.

WORD POWER

We know that all things work together for good to those who love God, to those who are the called according to His purpose.
ROMANS 8:28

May He grant you according to your heart's desire, and fulfill all your purpose.
PSALM 20:4

[I make] mention of you in my prayers: that the God of our Lord Jesus Christ, the Father of glory, may give to you the spirit of wisdom and revelation in the knowledge of Him, the eyes of your understanding being enlightened; that you may know what is the hope of His calling.
EPHESIANS 1:16–18

The gifts and the calling of God are irrevocable.
ROMANS 11:29

To everything there is a season, a time for every purpose under heaven.
ECCLESIASTES 3:1

6
Pray That Your Adult Children Will Work Successfully and Have Financial Stability

One of the most important things our adult children need to hear from God about is direction regarding their life's work. Without a leading from Him, they can struggle, flounder, and wander for years, going from job to job and from frustration to disappointment to doubt to despair. We also want them to find purpose in each job they do, even if that purpose is simply to cause them to say with certainty, "I'm going to go back to school and get more training or a new degree because I definitely don't want to end up doing this for the rest of my life." Or saying, "I'm going to take what I've learned at this job and apply it to the next." The point is to find that balance between gaining experience and wasting their time on something God is not blessing.

The first five chapters of this book talk about asking God to pour out His Spirit upon our adult children; to help them develop a heart for Him, His ways, and His Word; to give them wisdom, discernment, and revelation; to set them free so they can become all He made them to be; and to enable them to develop a clear sense of purpose. Praying in these five ways will lay a foundation in your adult children's lives that will not only help them to understand how God is *calling* them to serve Him, but will also reveal to them what their life's work is to be. Too often adult children can't find the *direction* God has for their lives with regard to their work because they don't hear from Him. Without a *God-given vision,* they will move aimlessly. Your prayers can help them to find all that.

Isaiah talked about how God would create a new heaven and a new earth, and the former one would not even be remembered (Isaiah 65:17). And in that day the life of the righteous (the believers) would not be cut off prematurely. And what you work for you will keep and not be robbed of it. "They shall build houses and inhabit them; they shall plant vineyards and eat their fruit . . . and *My elect shall long enjoy the work of their hands. They shall not labor in vain* . . . It shall come to pass that before they call, I will answer; and while they are still speaking, I will hear" (Isaiah 65:17–24, emphasis added).

God wants us to enjoy our work and not labor in vain. And that's what we all want as well. That's why we should pray, "Lord, You have said that Your desire for those who love You and live Your way is that we will long enjoy the work of our hands and that we should not labor in vain. I pray for my adult children that they will love You, live Your way, and understand what they are to do with their lives. I pray they will always enjoy the work of their hands and not waste precious time in labor that bears no fruit."

Pray That They Will Be Diligent and Work Hard

I have heard it said by people who own businesses that many young people today want to get paid, but they don't want to work hard and be diligent about their work. I know that's certainly not true for many, but there are some adult children who don't understand how valuable hard work is. When I was a teenager, I couldn't wait to get into the workforce and I wanted to work hard. And from the time I was 16 I have worked hard every year for the rest of my life. I think the reason for my dedication was because I had been raised poor and if I didn't work for it, I didn't have it.

The fact that some people have no interest in working hard is a mystery to me when there is so much to be gained — and not just monetarily. There is also great personal satisfaction and a sense of accomplishment that comes as a reward for the soul. But too many adult children have been given so much that they think, *Why work hard when I can get what I want for free?* Or they have a lazy spirit, which clouds their thinking. Or they have taken drugs, which clouds their souls.

Five Things the Bible Says About People Who Are Diligent and Work Hard

1. *Those who work hard will always have enough.* "He who has a slack hand becomes poor, but the hand of the diligent makes rich" (Proverbs 10:4).
2. *Those who work hard will possess a great inner treasure.* "The lazy man does not roast what he took in hunting, but diligence is man's precious possession" (Proverbs 12:27).
3. *Those who work hard will enrich their souls.* "The soul of a lazy man

desires, and has nothing; but the soul of the diligent shall be made rich" (Proverbs 13:4).

4. *Those who work hard will become leaders.* "The hand of the diligent will rule, but the lazy man will be put to forced labor" (Proverbs 12:24).
5. *Those who work hard will always be increasing.* "Wealth gained by dishonesty will be diminished, but he who gathers by labor will increase" (Proverbs 13:11).

These five reasons alone give us enough inspiration to pray for our adult children to work hard and be diligent. If they refuse, they are destined to end up with nothing.

If You Have a Child Who Can't — or Won't — Keep a Job

Adult children who can't *keep* a job or won't *get* a job usually do not have enough contact with God through personal prayer. I guarantee that if someone asks God for direction for their lives, especially in regard to their work, He will give it to them. They must be able to hear from God about this, because He can secure their professional direction and financial security in ways they cannot begin to do on their own. They must find out what they were created to do and get direction from the Lord as to how to go about doing it.

This is not to say that people who have the leading of the Lord will always work in fulfilling and purposeful jobs. We all have times when we work in jobs just to pay the bills, and there is nothing wrong with that. In fact, there is everything right with it, as long as we recognize the purpose in it and give thanks to God for it. No matter how meaningless the job we have appears to be, we can still be working *toward* something. We can work at a boring job if it is serving a purpose, such as to be able to put a child in a better school, to pay off a debt, to live in a safer area, to have money for further education, or whatever is meaningful for our lives. We can dedicate any job to God's glory, no matter how far away it seems to be from our dream job. When our adult children dedicate whatever they are doing to God's glory, He will bless it and bring much good out of it. He will see to it that each job adds to the other and builds toward something.

It helps if your adult children understand that "in all labor there is profit," even when they are not compensated as they would like, and that merely talking about working leads to poverty (Proverbs 14:23). When they don't see any purpose in the work they are doing, their hearts won't be in it and they will not do their jobs as well. It will deplete them instead of energizing them. But when they are serving God, even in menial jobs, they will have a sense of purpose that carries them through to better jobs and greater success.

If you have adult children who will not work, they are on a path that will eventually bring destruction. Don't allow them to go down that path. The Bible says, "The desire of the lazy man kills him, for his hands refuse to labor" (Proverbs 21:25). Pray that they will have the joy that comes from dedicating their work to the Lord and find the fulfillment of working to help others.

There is a difference between an adult child who won't get a job and wants to play more than work and because of that can't pay his rent, and an adult child who is working hard but business is extremely slow or he has been laid off because his employer is downsizing and now he can't make his mortgage payments. In the first scenario the child may have to fall in order to come to his senses. In the second situation, you can keep that adult child from being destroyed by helping him. Ask God to show you the truth.

If your adult child is getting financial assistance from you, or any other assistance from you for that matter, you have the right to talk to her (him) about what she (he) is doing with her (his) life. Pray first that she (he) will have a receptive heart and be open to hearing your input. Then pray that she (he) will be humble enough to honor you as a parent by listening to your advice. Do you remember the commandment that says children must honor their parents if they expect things to go well with them? (Exodus 20:12). You never know whether things are not going well in your adult child's work because she (he) has not honored you as a parent. Ask God to show you if you are giving your adult child so much assistance that she (he) doesn't have to try to be self-supporting. There is a point where *assisting* becomes *enabling,* and we need God to show us where to draw that line.

Pray for Them to Have Financial Stability

Along with praying about our adult children's work, we also need to pray about their finances. Pray that they have an income that meets their needs. An adult child with a spouse and four children needs more income than a single person sharing expenses with five roommates. As their needs increase, we have to always pray that their income rises with it. No matter what they do they want to be successful, and that will be reflected in how their income increases. Pray they will find balance so they don't have "a slack hand" and become poor (Proverbs 10:4) or "overwork to be rich" (Proverbs 23:4). Pray that they will work hard enough, and have opportunity enough, to bring in the income they need.

Of course, it's best to pray *before* anything happens, as a preventative measure. For example, pray for her (him) to have favor with the people *for* whom and with whom she (he) works. Pray for her (him) to be fairly and generously compensated for the work she (he) does. Pray that her (his) work will be appreciated and recognized, enabling her (him) to advance. Pray that she (he) is doing what she (he) is supposed to be doing at that time.

If your adult children are pursuing the wrong occupation — outside of the will of God — then they will continue to struggle. That is not to say they won't struggle in their work if they are *in* the will of God, but that struggle will lead to something great. When they are outside the will of God, the struggle will lead nowhere. Better to struggle while *in* the will of God and eventually bear fruit than to struggle *outside* of God's will and have nothing lasting to show for it.

Adult children with powerfully praying parents often find their life's work early, but that is certainly not always the case. There are many godly, devoted, praying parents who have been baffled at the lack of motivation in an adult child, especially when their other adult children are not that way. The answer as to what to do about that is to keep praying fervently and not give up. That child has a *great purpose,* and often it takes *great prayer* to see great purpose come forth.

Remember that the enemy will always come to oppose and resist what God's plans are for your adult child and try to impose his own plans. Let your prayers become a force that is a stopping point for that. Surrender any dreams and plans *you* may have for your adult child's life and pray for *God's* plan to rule over all. God's plans and your dreams may be one and the same, but you need to be sure. And you don't want yours to get in the way if they don't line up with God's.

God will ask us to lay down our dreams for our adult children because He wants both us and our adult children to depend on Him to make their lives happen.

God asked Abraham to take his only son, Isaac, to a specific place in order to offer him up as a sacrifice. Isaac was the child of God's promise to Abraham and Sarah, who had been childless into old age. God was asking Abraham to lay down his dream — his dream of having a son and his dream for what his son would become — and give that dream entirely to God. As it turned out, this was the same place where God would eventually sacrifice His only Son, Jesus. By being *willing* to make that sacrifice, Abraham showed his reverence, uncompromising love, and trust for God because he believed God would raise Isaac from the dead. God intervened just in time by providing a ram for the sacrifice instead of Isaac (Genesis 22:1–13). Then "Abraham called the name of the place, The-LORD-Will-Provide; as it is said to this day, 'In the Mount of the LORD it shall be provided' " (Genesis 22:14).

What this means for us is that God is faithful to provide for us when we have a need, if we are faithful to obey Him and follow His lead.

It also means that God requires us to lay down our dream — even when we know our vision is from *Him* — because He wants us to know that *He* is the one who will make it happen. When we let a dream die that is God's will, He will resurrect it. Then we will know for certain that *God* made it happen and we did not accomplish it on our own strength.

Pray that your adult child will be able to surrender her (his) dream to the Lord. And when the dream feels as good as dead, pray for God to resurrect it. Pray for your adult child to see the hand of God in it. This foreknowledge of God's ways will help you to not lose heart and become worried when you see financial struggle happen for your adult child. It will help you to be encouraging, even when he or she is discouraged, because you see the bigger picture.

Eight Ways to Pray for Financial Security

1. *Pray that your adult child will always work when the opportunity is there.* "He who sleeps in harvest is a son who causes shame" (Proverbs 10:5).
2. *Pray that your adult child will have wisdom to save money for lean times.* "He who gathers in summer is a wise son" (Proverbs 10:5).
3. *Pray that your adult child learns to give to the Lord what He requires and*

desires. " 'Bring all the tithes into the storehouse, that there may be food in My house, and try Me now in this,' says the LORD of hosts, 'If I will not open for you the windows of heaven and pour out for you such blessing that there will not be room enough to receive it' " (Malachi 3:10).

4. *Pray that your adult child will always give to the poor and needy.* "Blessed is he who considers the poor; the LORD will deliver him in time of trouble. The LORD will preserve him and keep him alive, and he will be blessed on the earth; you will not deliver him to the will of his enemies" (Psalm 41:1–2). "Whoever shuts his ears to the cry of the poor will also cry himself and not be heard" (Proverbs 21:13). "He who gives to the poor will not lack, but he who hides his eyes will have many curses" (Proverbs 28:27).
5. *Pray that your adult child will seek the Lord about everything, including God's provision.* "The young lions lack and suffer hunger; but those who seek the LORD shall not lack any good thing" (Psalm 34:10).

6. *Pray that your adult child gains wealth according to the will of God, so as not to lose the ability to enjoy it.* "The blessing of the LORD makes one rich, and He adds no sorrow with it" (Proverbs 10:22).
7. *Pray that your adult child will know that true treasure is found in the Lord.* "Where your treasure is, there your heart will be also" (Matthew 6:21).
8. *Pray that your adult child will always have a sense of what is right and ethical.* "As a partridge that broods but does not hatch, so is he who gets riches, but not by right; I will leave him in the midst of his days, and at his end he will be a fool" (Jeremiah 17:11).

The world economy is so unstable. There are no guarantees, except in God's economy. God says if you give, you will receive; if you seek His will, you will have all you need; if you work hard, you will be rewarded; if you live God's way, you will never go hungry. Our adult children need our prayers to help them understand and trust this principle of giving.

Always keep in mind as you pray that God sometimes uses finances — or *lack* thereof

— to get your adult child's attention. If you pray and pray and things don't change, ask God to show you and your adult child if there are important lessons that need to be learned through this. Or if perhaps God has other plans for her (him) that require some sort of change in occupation, job, lifestyle, focus, attitude, goals, or vision. As you pray about this, you will gain the confidence of knowing that your adult child is in God's hands. Perhaps God simply wants her (him) to understand where her (his) true treasure is before He blesses her (him) with monetary rewards.

We all have good times and not-so-good times when it comes to work and finances. If we are walking with God, then even setbacks will be nothing more than that. What we want to avoid are major disasters, such as losing a house, getting into debt, or filing for bankruptcy. Our prayers don't guarantee that our adult children will be able to avoid all financial difficulties, but you can trust that God will help them in such situations and teach them valuable lessons in the process.

How to Pray for an Adult Child Who Is Having Financial Problems

No one wants to see their adult children go through financial problems. Not only don't we want it for *them,* but we also don't want it for *us* either, for it will surely cost us something too. Often God will use financial problems to get a person's attention. And nothing does that faster or better, except for sickness. A financial problem is one of the greatest stresses in our lives, and it is just as stressful for us when we see it happening in our adult children.

We've all seen financial disasters happen because of health problems, divorce, children getting into trouble, or unemployment. And God will use these situations to get our attention. It may be that financial ruin, foreclosure, or bankruptcy is the only way to get your children on the right path. They may have to fall so that they come to see God as their source. Pray and ask God to show you the truth about that. He will. No one wants to experience financial difficulty, but it could lead to a complete turnaround in an adult child.

If your adult children have already experienced financial disaster — whether due to careless spending or they have fallen on hard times, whether they are in the struggling stage or they have lost their home and filed for bankruptcy — know that God can bring them back, put them on solid ground, and give them financial stability again. Pray that their situation will turn them to the Lord and His ways more than ever before in their lives.

If the financial disaster or trouble is caused because an adult child won't work — whether it is due to a serious lack of confidence, fear of failure, depression, self-centeredness, or laziness — he (she) needs the professional help of a financial counselor and perhaps a Christian counselor. This is a problem that won't go away without intervention, especially if there is a pattern of behavior. If an adult child is a hard worker to the point of being a workaholic and important things are being sacrificed, such as health, marriage, children, and time with the Lord, then pray for an awakening in him (her) to understand the need for balance and a sense of God-ordained priorities.

One of the advantages of losing everything is that it forces you to realize that *God is everything.* And *He will provide everything.* And *in Him everything* is *found.* And *everything you have comes from Him.* "My God shall supply all your need according to His riches in glory by Christ Jesus" (Philippians

4:19). Becoming totally dependant upon God will help your adult children to clear the slate and start over. It will lead them to find the right work. It will give them wisdom with spending and saving and living within their means. With enough prayer — and praise to God that He is doing great things in the midst of this situation — this could be the best thing that ever happened to them. It could be the catalyst that thrusts them onto the right track.

The best thing to do is to start praying about financial stability *before* anything bad happens. However, if it is too late for prevention prayer now, pray a redemption prayer instead. Remember that God can redeem everything — even our adult children and their financial problems.

Lord, I pray Your blessings upon (name of adult child). Bless the work of her (his) hands in every way. Give her (him) a strong sense of purpose so that she (he) is led to the right occupation and is always in the job or position that is Your will for her (his) life. Speak to her (him) about what she (he) was created to do, so that she (he) never wanders from job to job without a purpose. Help her (him) find great purpose in every job she (he) does.

Help her (him) to be diligent in everything and never succumb to a lazy or careless attitude. Where there is any kind of a laziness or fear holding her (him) back, I pray for a breaking of that stronghold. Pour out Your Holy Spirit upon her (him) and give her (him) the wisdom to rise up out of that deception and have the strength to walk free of those paralyzing chains. Help her (him) to be "not lagging in diligence, fervent in spirit, serving the Lord" (Romans 12:11).

I pray that she (he) will always do her (his) work for Your glory (Colossians 3:23). Convict her (his) heart if there is ever any temptation to do anything unethical, whether deliberately or unknowingly. Lead her (him) away from all questionable or illegal actions. Help her (him) to always know that whatever gain appears to be hers (his) by unlawful or unethical actions will never be kept, and it will ruin her (his) reputation in the end. I pray that she (he) will be convinced that a good reputation is far more valuable than riches (Jeremiah 17:11).

Give my adult children wisdom regarding all money matters. Help them to see danger before anything serious happens. Give them understanding about spending, saving, and investing wisely. Help them to not make stupid or careless mistakes. Protect them so that their finances are not lost, stolen, or wasted. I pray that the enemy will never be allowed to steal, kill, or destroy anything in their lives. I pray for my adult children that they "do good, that they be rich in good works, ready to give, willing to share, storing up for themselves a good foundation for the time to come, that they may lay hold on eternal life" (1 Timothy 6:18–19).

Lord, help my adult children to commit their finances to You so that You will be in charge of them. Help them to get free of debt and be careful with their spending so that their future is secure. Enable them to be good stewards of all you have given them. Help them to learn to give to You in a way that is pleasing in Your sight.

Where my adult child is having financial problems right now, I pray for things to turn around. Help her (him) to learn from the correction and instruction of wise teachers and people of maturity, wisdom, and experience, so that she (he) will avoid poverty and embarrassment and gain honor and prosperity (Proverbs 13:18). By the power of the Holy Spirit, I speak God's blessing of provision upon (name of adult child). Give her (him) wisdom with regard to work, career, occupation, and profession. I pray for success in the work you have called her (him) to do. Open the doors of opportunity and help her (him) to find favor in the workplace. Help her (him) to be fairly compensated for the work she (he) does.

Lord, You have said to "seek the kingdom of God, and all these things shall be added to you" (Luke 12:31). Help my adult children to make seeking You their first priority so they can establish financial stability. Help them to surrender to You in body, mind, soul, and spirit so they can move into the abundance and prosperity You have for them. I pray that the beauty of the Lord will be upon them and establish the work of their hands (Psalm 90:17). I pray that they will "long enjoy the work of their hands" and that "they shall not labor in vain" (Isaiah 65:22–23).

In Jesus' name I pray.

WORD POWER

Whatever you do, do it heartily, as to the Lord and not to men.
COLOSSIANS 3:23

Every man should eat and drink and enjoy the good of all his labor — it is the gift of God.
ECCLESIASTES 3:13

Commit your works to the LORD, and your thoughts will be established.
PROVERBS 16:3

I have been young, and now am old; yet I have not seen the righteous forsaken, nor his descendants begging bread.
PSALM 37:25

Do not seek what you should eat or what you should drink, nor have an anxious mind. For all these things the nations of the world seek after, and your Father knows that you need these things. But seek the kingdom of God, and all these things shall be added to you.
LUKE 12:29–31

7
Pray That Your Adult Children Will HAVE A SOUND MIND AND A RIGHT ATTITUDE

None of us really knows what another person is thinking. Very few people, if any, share their every thought with someone else. Not even husbands and wives; not even in close relationships between parents and adult children. The truth is, only God knows all of our thoughts. That's why He is the One to go to regarding what goes on in the mind and emotions of your adult child.

Some of the greatest struggles many of our adult children have to face are those that happen in their minds. The enemy will always try to get them to believe his lies and reject God's truth. He knows that as long as they believe his lies, he has won. We all can have thoughts that plague us by playing over and over in our heads, even causing manifestations in our physical bodies, such as pain, nausea, disease, or the inability of our bodies to do what they are supposed to do.

Our thoughts can not only make us sick

in our body, but in our minds and emotions as well. One wrong thought can cause us to fail in life, if we believe a lie about ourselves instead of what the Word of God says about us. For example, if we constantly say, "I always fail at everything" instead of "I can do all things through Christ who strengthens me," we are more likely to experience failure. The problem is that too often we believe the lie *is* the truth because we are not clear on what God's truth is. And we hear the screaming voice of the enemy to our minds, which is so much louder than the still, small voice of God to our souls. The Bible says of the enemy that "there is no truth in him . . . for he is a liar and the father of it" (John 8:44).

Everyone is susceptible to that kind of mental torment, but our adult children even more so. Because no matter how much noise, distraction, and worldly input we were exposed to growing up, they have had much worse. They have every kind of electronic devise vying for their attention. Some young adults have had their ears, eyes, and minds plugged into something other than the Lord for years. Whatever captures their eyes and ears will also capture their minds and hearts.

Suicides or murderous rampages of teenagers and young adults all begin as a seed of a lie planted in their minds through their eyes or ears, and it festers and grows silently in the dark parts of their soul. Negative emotions such as anger, hurt, rejection, fear, anxiety, and loneliness, all fuel and feed the lie so it can grow until it is out of control. A person who believes he is rejected will become hurt, anxious, and fearful, then lonely and isolated, and finally angry. All of these negative aspects of his personality will cause people to reject him even more. And so the lie grows until it becomes not only self-destructive but destructive of other people as well.

Our adult children can have lies playing in their minds that limit their ability to think clearly and accurately about themselves and their circumstances. They can end up believing lies such as:

1. No one likes me.
2. I am rejected by the people I want to accept me.
3. I can't do anything right.
4. I'm not good at anything.
5. I'm a failure.
6. No one cares about me.
7. It doesn't matter what I do.
8. There is nothing I can do to change

things.

9. God doesn't hear my prayers.
10. God doesn't care about me.

When your adult children have negative thoughts and believe lies like the ones above, these thoughts can push them toward the very thing they feared — failure and rejection. We must pray for our adult children's eyes to be opened to see that these kinds of thoughts are not God giving them revelation for their lives. It is the enemy speaking lies to their souls and they are accepting them as truth.

These thoughts appear to be harmless at first, but when they are held up to the light of God's truth in His Word, the lie is exposed for what it is. One of the tactics of the enemy is to try to steal God's truth from your adult children by getting them to question the Bible. He will bring contradictions into their minds about the reliability of God's Word. "Is the Bible really inspired by God or just men?" "Does God really mean that?" They don't recognize that what they are being drawn into mentally is from the enemy. "There is a way that seems right to a man, but its end is the way of death" (Proverbs 14:12). They think they are being open minded when they question God's

Word. The question is, open minded to what? And to whom? Too often an adult child is open to enemy *intrusion* into his mind instead of God's *infusion* into his entire being.

Things That Are True About a Believer's Mind

All sin begins as a thought in the mind. "From within, out of the heart of men, proceed evil thoughts, adulteries, fornications, murders, thefts, covetousness, wickedness, deceit, lewdness, an evil eye, blasphemy, pride, foolishness" (Mark 7:21–22). If we don't take control of our minds, the devil will. It is the same for our adult children, only they have to fight harder to resist it. Our generation had to seek out sin if we were inclined to do so. Our adult children have it thrown in their faces every day, and they have to wade through it or do all they can to rise above it. They need the help and enablement of the Lord and our prayers. Praying for your adult children can quiet the enemy's voice to their souls and help them better identify and control the thoughts they allow into their minds.

Three Things That Are True About the Mind of a Believer

1. God gives each of us a sound mind.
2. The enemy wants to destroy our sound minds with his lies.
3. We have a choice about what we allow into our minds. We can control what we think.

Three Points of Prayer for the Minds of Our Adult Children

1. Pray that your adult children have nothing less than the sound minds God has given them.
2. Pray that the enemy of their souls cannot fill their minds with lies that oppress them mentally and emotionally.
3. Pray that your adult children make the right choices as to what they allow into their minds.

We are not trying to practice some kind of mind control exercises here. We are doing some God-be-in-control exercises. Through our prayers we want to erect a barrier against anything that opposes the sound minds that God gives us all.

I know an adult child — actually, I've known a number of adult children just like her — who believed many lies about herself. She believed she wasn't smart, talented, or attractive. She felt that no man would even want her because of that. If you were to meet her and talk to her, you would know that none of that is true and you would be surprised to hear she even believed such things about herself. However, those beliefs kept her from moving forward in her life for a long time. They kept her from being hopeful, and so she became depressed, reclusive, and isolated. She expected to fail and be rejected because it appeared to her that everything she did ended in failure.

When her mother invited her into a weekly prayer group, they began to pray over her on a regular basis about breaking the control of these negative, troubling, and defeating thoughts. They prayed that her eyes would be opened to the truth and that the lies of the enemy to her mind and heart would be exposed and their power broken. They prayed that she would be free to hear the truth about herself from the Holy Spirit.

The answers to these prayers didn't happen overnight, but eventually all that negative thinking and acceptance of lies about herself was finally broken and she began to change. She became more open, outgoing, and happy. She started thinking less about herself and more about others. Good things began to happen to her, and doors opened to a new and better career. Today she is hopeful about her life and happy with whom God made her to be.

So many adult children are the way she was. And without prayer support and being able to identify the lies, they will continue believing that the lies from the enemy are true and the truth of God's Word is a lie.

Adult children who are raised to be very solid and straight thinkers can still become oppressed in their minds and emotions by the enemy. I know of a young man raised in a strong Christian home who entertained thoughts of suicide because the young woman with whom he was seriously contemplating marriage had broken off their relationship. Rejection is hard for anyone to take — especially from someone so important in their life — but the enemy can get into that kind of situation and inject self-destructive thoughts.

We naturally do not want to destroy ourselves. We are built for preservation. God created us with the desire to stay alive. It is the enemy who comes and blinds our eyes so that we think there is no other way out and suicide is the only option. Of course, this is an extreme example — yet not the most extreme. The most extreme are those who kill others and *then* take their own lives. I'm not saying your adult child will ever fall into the category of contemplating suicide for any reason, but I am saying that the enemy of your adult child's soul will always try to get him or her to that point. And that's why we must pray for our adult children to be free of all enemy oppression.

Pray That They Make the Right Choices About What They Allow into Their Minds

We all have a choice as to what we allow into our minds. Pray that your adult child will understand that and make the right choices. Again, the first five chapters of this book will effect this. If God answers those prayers for your adult children and pours out His Spirit upon them, draws them close to Himself and His ways, makes His Word come alive to their hearts, gives them wisdom and discernment, sets them free from anything that keeps them from becoming all He made them to be, and gives them a sense of His purpose for their lives, then they are far more likely to make good choices about what they allow into their minds.

Because of the terrible assault on their minds, our adult children need the reinforcement our prayers can give them. An adult child who has a clear mind and is free of negative emotions can accomplish great things.

Dissolving a Bad Attitude

A bad attitude is something people can have without even realizing it. A person thinks he is just having private inner thoughts, yet people pick up on attitude, even if they don't know exactly what it is.

One adult child told me that she struggled with having a critical attitude toward others. She said that finding fault in others caused her to feel better about herself. It was a defense mechanism whereby she built herself up as she tore others down in her mind. Even though she never spoke her criticism, it permeated her personality and caused a divide between her and others, limiting her friendships. I told her to pray every day and ask God to set her free from this and help her to feel better about herself and more appreciative of others.

As she prayed, the Holy Spirit showed her how prideful and mean spirited she had been. She saw how her attitude was not pleasing to God, and that He would not bless a critical spirit. She eventually was liberated from that terrible critical attitude — which was destroying her — and her demeanor completely changed. People now feel comfortable around her, and she has the kind of close friendships she always wanted and was unable to sustain before.

One of the things we can do to help our adult children get free of negative attitudes is to get free from them ourselves. (Remember, I talked about parents getting free in chapter 4?) If we can get rid of our anger, anxiety, fear, pride, or critical spirit — all of which contribute to a bad attitude — we pave the way for our adult children to recognize their own bad attitudes and get free of them too. If we are in bondage to any kind of negative emotion, our adult children can pick that up. If we get free of bad attitudes, wrong thoughts, or negative emotions today, they can be benefactors of that today as well.

The fact that Jesus died and rose again guarantees us a shared inheritance with Him of all that Father God has for His children who believe in Him and receive Jesus as Savior. That's us. The eternal inheritance we receive from our heavenly Father is ultimately a glorious life with Him forever. But we also inherit His goodness, grace, love, peace, joy, and power right now. We inherit His sound mind and freedom from negative emotions. And so do our adult children. Whether they open up to receive all that depends on whether their hearts are open to the things of God and they recognize all He has for them. That's why we must pray for them to hear from God and be open to His Spirit working in their lives.

I know a mother who was extremely fearful about everything when she was raising her children. Her daughter is now fearful about everything while raising hers. It's one thing to have fear about something bad happening to your child — every parent has that to some degree — but when fear paralyzes you and controls your life, making you and others around you miserable, it has become a "spirit of fear." Both mother and daughter are believers, but they have never known freedom in Christ in this area. They don't understand that fear is a spirit that brings torment. Fear that takes over your life is never from God. If this mother were to ask God to set her free from all fear, He would do that. And this would in turn help her daughter to believe for God's delivering power to set her free from fear as well.

We must ask God to set *us* and our adult

children free from any wrong attitudes, and help us to see our lives from His perspective.

FIVE NEGATIVE EMOTIONS AND BAD ATTITUDES TO AVOID

1. *Pray that your adult child is free of pride.* "A man's pride will bring him low, but the humble in spirit will retain honor" (Proverbs 29:23). Pride has built-in consequence and will bring your adult child down faster than anything else. Satan was brought down by pride, and so will everyone else be. That's because God hates pride. He *resists* the proud and gives grace to the humble (James 4:6). Pray that pride will not take over your adult children and destroy their lives.
2. *Pray that your adult child is free of fear.* "God has not given us a spirit of fear, but of power and of love and of a sound mind" (2 Timothy 1:7). Fear does not come from the Lord. It is a spirit from the enemy's camp. God gives us love, power, and soundness of mind. God says, "perfect love casts out fear" (1 John

4:18). Pray that the perfect love of God in your adult child's heart and soul will evaporate all fear in his (her) mind, so he (she) can enjoy the love, power, and soundness of mind God has for him (her).

3. *Pray that your adult child is free of anger.* "An angry man stirs up strife, and a furious man abounds in transgression" (Proverbs 29:22). A person who gives place to anger will always stir up strife in every relationship with actions or words. Even the people with whom he (she) is *not* angry will sense an angry spirit and be uncomfortable around it. Pray that your adult child never gives place to anger.
4. *Pray that your adult child is free of anxiety.* "Anxiety in the heart of man causes depression, but a good word makes it glad" (Proverbs 12:25). Worry and anxiety deplete our lives. God did not create us to be able to live with anxiety. He says we are not to be anxious about *anything,* but to come to Him in prayer about *everything* so we can have peace (Philippians 4:6–7). Pray for your adult child to be able to do

exactly that so he (she) will not have anxiety and depression.

5. *Pray that your adult child is free of a broken heart.* "He heals the brokenhearted and binds up their wounds" (Psalm 147:3). There is healing for anyone whose heart is broken and their soul is wounded. Being brokenhearted is terribly damaging, and especially so if God isn't invited in to mend and heal. Pray that your adult children will be healed of any brokenheartedness they experience. Without that healing, they can develop an attitude of self-pity or self-protection.

There are many other negative emotions, such as: hopelessness, insecurity, confusion, doubt, depression, and loneliness, that require the healing touch of God. Ask the Lord to show you any negative emotion or wrong attitude your adult child has and pray for him (her) to be free of it.

Praise Heals the Mind, Emotions, and Attitudes

One of the most powerful things we can do in our lives to get rid of negative emotions, turmoil in our minds, and wrong attitudes is to worship and praise God. No matter what is happening in our lives, or in the lives of our adult children, God is always worthy of our praise. Praising Him invites His presence to reign in our midst. And transformation is found in the presence of God.

It's important to remember the good things God has done in our lives and to remind our adult children of those things as well. That will help them to connect with the goodness of God and dwell on it. In the book of Esther it is said that the Jews decided that they would regularly remember and celebrate how they defeated their enemies, "that these days should be remembered and kept throughout every generation, *every family* . . . and that the memory of them should not perish among their descendants" (Esther 9:28, emphasis added). We parents of adult children need to do the same. We must openly give thanks and praise to God for the great things He has done in our lives. "One generation shall praise Your works to another, and shall declare Your mighty acts" (Psalm 145:4). We need to tell them how God set us free from the enemy of our souls and minds, and how He can do the same for them.

In addition to that, it is good to tell your adult children about the consequences of sin in people's lives when you see it happening in the world. Just as God spoke through Joel saying, "Tell your children about it, let your children tell their children, and their children another generation" (Joel 1:3). They need to know that sin opens us up to the enemy's attacks. But remind them of the promises of God in His Word to bring us back from sin so we can find healing and restoration. Speak the Word of God to your adult children whenever you can. If they are worried, tell them that no weapon formed against them will prosper when they live God's way (Isaiah 54:17).

You may no longer have authority over your children, but you do have authority over all the power of the enemy. Negative thoughts, emotions, and attitudes can be a ploy of the enemy to destroy a person by causing a torment of the soul that is very real and serious. And a person can deliberately invite the enemy in with their own disobedience and rebelliousness. Rebellion begins as a bad attitude that never gets corrected. It becomes more and more established as it is continually given place to in their lives. The Bible says that rebellion is like "the sin of witchcraft" (1 Samuel 15:23). Rebellion is the path to personal destruction. A right attitude has no rebellion whatsoever attached to it. Pray that your adult child will resist a rebellious attitude and instead have a spirit of praise and worship.

Keep in mind that God *in us* is far greater than the enemy and his plans. "You are of God, little children, and have overcome them, because He who is *in you* is greater than he who is in the world" (1 John 4:4, emphasis added). We must always remind our adult children of that, and pray that this truth will take root in their hearts. Remind them that because we are believers, "we have the mind of Christ" (1 Corinthians 2:16). Pray that they will settle for nothing less.

PRAYER POWER

Lord, I pray that You would help (name of adult child) to be able to take control of his (her) mind and emotions. Enable him (her) to bring every thought into captivity (2 Corinthians 10:5). Help him (her) to not entertain just any thought that comes into his (her) head, but to have the discernment to recognize the voice of the enemy speaking lies. Take away all deception so that he (she) will not accept a lie for truth. Help him (her) to clearly recognize the enemy's deception for the purpose of destroying him (her).

Give him (her) the ability to resist filling his (her) mind with anything that is not glorifying to You. Help him (her) to be repulsed by vile and unedifying books, magazines, music, films, and Internet and television images so that he (she) always turns away from those things. Help him (her) to instead fill his (her) mind with thoughts that please You. Help him (her) to think about things that are true, noble, just, pure, lovely, good, virtuous, and praiseworthy (Philippians 4:8). Help him (her) to fill his (her) mind with "the best, not the worst; the beautiful, not the ugly; things to praise, not things to curse" (Philippians 4:8, MSG).

I pray for my adult child to be able to

resist any attempt of the enemy to torment his (her) mind with negative thoughts and emotions. Help him (her) to choose the love, power, and sound mind You have given him (her). Dissolve any dark clouds of negative emotions that hover over him (her). Set him (her) free from all confusion and bring clarity of mind. Let the mind of Christ be in him (her) (Philippians 2:5). Help him (her) to be renewed in the spirit of his (her) mind (Ephesians 4:23).

Dissolve all pride and bring humility. Take away rebellion and bring repentance. Remove all anxiety and worry and bring peace. Give him (her) faith to replace all doubt. Bring Your joy where there is sadness or depression. Give him (her) confidence in You to replace insecurity within himself (herself). Give him (her) peace, patience, and forgiveness to replace all anger. Give him (her) Your love to dissolve all fear. Give him (her) Your presence to erase all loneliness.

I pray that You would give him (her) wisdom about what he (she) allows into his (her) mind. Give him (her) great discernment so the lines between good and bad are clearly seen. Convict him (her) whenever he (she) crosses the line, and grieve his (her) spirit the way it grieves Yours. I pray for his (her) mind to be captured by You. Wherever his (her) mind and emotions have been captured by anything that is not of You, I pray that You would enable him (her) to silence the voice of the enemy by speaking Your truth. Teach him (her) to lift up praise and worship to You until he (she) hears Your voice clearly speaking to his (her) soul.

If ever my adult child has been ridiculed, humiliated, or made to feel less than what You made him (her) to be, I pray that You would heal those wounds and erase the scars. Keep him (her) from being imprisoned or hindered by bad memories. If I have said or done anything to make my adult child feel less than who You made him (her) to be, and this has kept him (her) from moving forward in life, I ask for Your forgiveness. Help me to forgive myself and enable my adult child to forgive me too. If I have had negative emotions that have caused my son (daughter) to be susceptible to the same thing, I pray for us both to be set free from that.

I know that "death and life are in the power of the tongue" (Proverbs 18:21), so I pray that You would help me to always speak words of life to my adult child's mind and heart whenever I talk to him (her). Enable me to build him (her) up and show love in ways he (she) can perceive. Help me to remind him (her) of all the good things God has done in his (her) life.

Lord, draw my adult child to Your Word so that it will be "a discerner of the thoughts and intents of the heart" every time he (she) reads it (Hebrews 4:12). Reveal to him (her) any wrong thinking or beliefs. Make Your thoughts to be his (her) thoughts. Help him (her) to have the "mind of Christ" at all times (1 Corinthian 2:16).

Where my adult children are struggling in their minds or emotions, I pray that You would extend peace to them like a river (Isaiah 66:12). To my adult children I pray that "the peace of God, which surpasses all understanding, will guard your hearts and minds through Christ Jesus" (Philippians 4:7). "Let the peace of God rule in your hearts . . . and be thankful" (Colossians 3:15).

In Jesus' name I pray.

Do not be conformed to this world, but be transformed by the renewing of your mind, that you may prove what is that good and acceptable and perfect will of God.
ROMANS 12:2

Let this mind be in you which was also in Christ Jesus.
PHILIPPIANS 2:5

This I say, therefore, and testify in the Lord, that you should no longer walk as the rest of the Gentiles walk, in the futility of their mind, having their understanding darkened, being alienated from the life of God, because of the ignorance that is in them, because of the blindness of their heart.
EPHESIANS 4:17–18

You will keep him in perfect peace, whose mind is stayed on You, because he trusts in You.
ISAIAH 26:3

Be anxious for nothing, but in everything by prayer and supplication, with thanksgiving, let your requests be

made known to God; and the peace of
God, which surpasses all
understanding, will guard your hearts
and minds through Christ Jesus.
PHILIPPIANS 4:6–7

8
Pray That Your Adult Children Will Resist Evil Influences and Destructive Behavior

Anyone walking through this culture in these times is going to bump up against evil influences. Unless they are a total recluse, it's impossible not to. If our adult children are not deliberately watchful and aware, their minds and hearts can download social and spiritual viruses that can damage their lives before they even know what is happening.

When evil influences overwhelm our adult children, they can become entrapped by destructive behavior from such things as alcohol, drugs, eating disorders, promiscuity, pornography, and much more that can destroy their lives. It used to be that bad kids from bad families did bad things and got into serious trouble. Now it can be good kids from good families who are enticed into doing terrible and destructive things.

No matter how good a parent you have been, your adult children can still be impacted by the dark side of today's culture. We must keep in mind that the magnetic draw of the evil forces of this world is strong and presents a constant battle for our children. We have to continually pray that they will be strong enough to resist this unrelenting encroachment of the enemy into their lives.

Earlier in this book I talked about the powerful Scripture verse that says all of our children will be taught by the Lord (Isaiah 54:13). A few verses later it says about those of us who believe that " '*no weapon formed against you shall prosper . . . This is the heritage of the servants of the LORD,* and their righteousness is from Me,' says the LORD" (Isaiah 54:17, emphasis added). This is worth repeating so that we will not forget.

We inherit our righteousness from *the Lord. He* is our righteousness. And that righteousness combats evil influences. However, righteousness doesn't just happen without prayer. We first have to pray in order to receive Jesus and His righteousness. Then we have to pray to receive *all* God has for us. We are not praying to *earn* something; we are praying to *receive* something. Without prayer — which is communicating with God — these things don't just happen. We can't assume that no weapon formed against us will ever prosper, because believe me it will. God's promises don't automatically happen without us doing our part. If we are not praying, the enemy is waiting to attack and destroy.

Jesus knew that Satan was attacking Simon Peter, and so He prayed for Peter to have the faith to withstand it. "Simon, Simon! Indeed, Satan has asked for you, that he may sift you as wheat. But I have prayed for you, *that your faith should not fail*" (Luke 22:31–32, emphasis added). Jesus could have said, "Satan, get lost," and been done with it, but He recognized that having *faith* and being able to *resist* was part of Peter's responsibility. If Jesus had to pray that His own disciple's faith would not fail in the midst of Satan's attack, how much more do we need to pray that our adult children's faith will not fail when *they* are being attacked? When the enemy comes to tempt them away from what God has for them, we can pray that they will have strong faith in God and His power on their behalf.

Jesus instructed His disciples to "pray that you may not enter into temptation" (Luke 22:40). We must instruct our adult children in the same way. We should rebuke the enemy on their behalf in Jesus' name, but they also must have strong faith to pray and resist temptation and whatever else the enemy throws at them.

Evil influences can confront even the most committed believer. Jesus prayed for His disciples to be protected from the enemy. He said to His heavenly Father, "I do not pray that You should take them out of the world, but that You should keep them from the evil one" (John 17:15). The disciples had walked with Jesus for three years and had seen His miracles and heard His preaching and teaching from the Word of God about the Father's kingdom, and yet they still needed to be prayed for in order to be protected from the enemy.

Jesus didn't say to His disciples, "I taught you the best I could, but you're on your own now, so good luck." Even though Jesus had prepared His disciples, He still prayed, "Keep them from the evil one." We parents must do no less. We must pray, "Lord, protect my children from the evil one."

When It's Not Their Fault

When evil penetrates your adult child's life and bad things happen through no fault of their own, because they have been living the Lord's way, you can trust that God will bless them in it. The story of Joseph is the perfect example of that. His story of evil happening *to* you is about as bad as it gets, but God totally redeemed his situation.

Because of the jealousy and evil in his brothers' hearts, they sold Joseph into slavery and he was taken to Egypt. But because Joseph was godly and faithful, God worked in all the evil that came against him. The most important thing that was true of Joseph was that *the Lord was with him.* Others saw that and rewarded him. "*The LORD was with Joseph* . . . and his master saw that *the LORD was with him* and that the *LORD made all he did to prosper* in his hand. So Joseph found favor in his sight, and served him. Then he made him overseer of his house, and all that he had he put under his authority" (Genesis 39:2–4, emphasis added). From that time on, "the LORD blessed the Egyptian's house for Joseph's sake; and the blessing of the LORD was on all that he had in the house and in the field" (Genesis 39:5).

But again, Joseph was victimized because of another person's evil and sin.

Joseph's master's wife tried to seduce him, but he did the right thing and refused to do anything wicked in God's eyes. She then lied and accused him of trying to molest her, and he was thrown in prison (Genesis 39:11–20). Still — in prison — "the LORD was with Joseph and *showed him mercy,* and He *gave him favor* in the sight of the keeper of the prison . . . *because the LORD was with him;* and *whatever he did, the LORD made it prosper*" (Genesis 39:21,23, emphasis added).

Whenever evil came against Joseph, he refused to compromise God's laws, and so the Lord was with him in everything he did. God not only turned things around for Joseph, but He eventually elevated him to second in command over all of Egypt. He ended up completely forgiving his brothers and saving his own family from disaster. He said to the brothers — who were very repentant for what they had done — "You meant evil against me; but God meant it for good" (Genesis 50:20). It wasn't God's will to see Joseph put into slavery, falsely accused, and jailed, but God worked through the situation to prosper him and eventually to position him to do the thing for which he was created.

If your adult child is enduring an undeserved punishment or hardship of some kind because of the evil or sin of others, pray that she (he) will not turn against the Lord but will instead draw closer to Him and praise Him in the situation. Pray that she (he) will stand strong in the ways of the

Lord, so that God will prosper and bless her (him). God works powerfully in the midst of an obedient and grateful heart to turn things around and do a miracle. Ask God to work through your adult child's difficult situation and use the evil done against her (him) for good. Most of all, pray for your adult child to always do the right thing, no matter how unfair life seems.

If your adult child is paying a very steep price right now for someone else's sin and evil, know that in the Bible God's people "found grace in the wilderness" (Jeremiah 31:2). Pray that your adult child will not only survive the unfair consequences, but while going through it she (he) will also find God's grace even in a terrible situation that seems to be barren of life.

Jesus was innocent, and He prayed to not have to go through what was ahead of Him. But He also prayed that God's will would be done and not His own (Luke 22:42). When He surrendered His will to His heavenly Father, "then an angel appeared to Him from heaven, strengthening Him" (Luke 22:43). Strength came from heaven to get Him through what He was facing. Ask God to send strength from heaven to help your adult child get through what she (he) is facing.

When It *Is* Their Fault

If your adult child is having to face some stiff consequences for *not* resisting evil influences and destructive behavior, pray that she (he) will learn a needed lesson without being destroyed. Pray that no matter what it is she (he) has to face as a result of her (his) actions, that God will strengthen her (him) to get through it. Pray that she (he) will be repentant and surrender to the will of God completely. God rewards a humble, repentant, submissive, dependent heart. No matter what happens, your adult child has a future of purpose that is well worth praying fervently about now.

Adam and Eve's first child was Cain and the second was Abel. God was not happy with what Cain offered to Him as a sacrifice because it was clearly an act of disobedience. Cain was angry about that, but God said to him, "Why are you angry? If you do the right thing, you will find favor with Me. But if you *don't* do the right thing, sin is waiting to own you. But you should rule over it" (Genesis 4:6–7, paraphrased).

God gave Cain a choice. He could choose to do the right thing and rule over sin, and therefore please God. Or he could choose *not* to do the right thing and allow his own jealousy (sin), anger (sin), and revenge (sin) to rule over him. He chose the latter, and he killed his brother Abel in a jealous rage. When God asked Cain what happened to his brother, Cain lied and said he didn't know. Lying to God is not a good idea. Especially since He already knows the truth. The only thing God wants to know when He asks a question is how *you* choose to answer. Too bad Cain didn't figure that out.

After Cain lied, God told him from that point on he would be cursed as a fugitive. But even then God in His mercy would not allow anyone to destroy him. Instead, God allowed Cain — an adult child who murdered his own brother — to still go on to have a family with children and grandchildren and great-grandchildren. God punished him, but He didn't give up on Cain completely. There were still many blessings in his life, even after his terrible sin.

We can't give up on our adult children either, no matter what they have done. We certainly don't have to condone or excuse their actions, enable them to continue in their sins, or cover for them so they don't suffer any consequences, but we should not give up praying for them. We must continue to believe in the potential God has put in them, even if we can't see it at the moment.

Pray for a humble, repentant, and teachable spirit in your adult child.

King David did so many things wrong. He committed adultery and murder. He lied and made terrible errors in judgment. And he could not manage his own home and children. Still, God said of David that he was "a man after My own heart, who will do all My will" (Acts 13:22). Obviously, "the LORD looks at the heart" (1 Samuel 16:7).

It wasn't that David never did anything wrong or never made a mistake. It was that he was quick to humble himself before God and repent. And because he had a teachable spirit, he learned from all of his mistakes and poor judgment, and he changed his ways. He paid a price for each sin, and yet he did not reject the correction of the Lord. "My son, do not despise the chastening of the LORD, nor detest His correction; for whom the LORD loves He corrects, just as a father the son in whom he delights" (Proverbs 3:11–12).

These stories prove that the love and grace of God are there for our adult children — no matter what they have done — to bring redemption and restoration. And that is how we should pray — for a repentant heart and a transformation in our adult children's lives. And we should thank God for His grace, which *gives* us *more* than we deserve and *doesn't punish* us *as much* as we deserve.

Seven Ways to Pray for Your Adult Child to Resist Evil Influences

1. *Pray that God will open your adult child's eyes to see the truth and not be blinded by the enemy.* "Even if our gospel is veiled, it is veiled to those who are perishing, whose minds the god of this age has blinded, who do not believe, lest the light of the gospel of the glory of Christ, who is the image of God, should shine on them" (2 Corinthians 4:3–4).
2. *Pray that your adult child can hear God's voice leading them.* "Your ears shall hear a word behind you, saying, 'This is the way, walk in it,' whenever you turn to the right hand or whenever you turn to the left" (Isaiah 30:21).
3. *Pray that your adult child's heart will be filled with wisdom and knowledge.* "When wisdom enters your heart, and knowledge is pleasant to your soul, discretion will preserve you;

understanding will keep you, to deliver you from the way of evil" (Proverbs 2:10–12).

4. *Pray that your adult child will turn away from evil.* "It may be that the house of Judah will hear all the adversities which I purpose to bring upon them, that everyone may turn from his evil way, that I may forgive their iniquity and their sin" (Jeremiah 36:3).
5. *Pray that your adult child will understand that she (he) is in a spiritual battle.* "We do not wrestle against flesh and blood, but against principalities, against powers, against the rulers of the darkness of this age, against spiritual hosts of wickedness in the heavenly places" (Ephesians 6:12).
6. *Pray that your adult child's trials will turn them to God.* "I am weary with my groaning; all night I make my bed swim; I drench my couch with my tears. My eye wastes away because of grief; it grows old because of all my enemies. Depart from me, all you workers of iniquity; for the LORD has heard the voice of my weeping. The LORD has heard my

supplication; the LORD will receive my prayer" (Psalm 6:6–9).

7. *Pray that your adult child will learn to praise God for the healing and deliverance He has for her (him).* "He sent His word and healed them, and delivered them from their destructions. Oh, that men would give thanks to the LORD for His goodness, and for His wonderful works to the children of men! Let them sacrifice the sacrifices of thanksgiving, and declare His works with rejoicing" (Psalm 107:20–22).

If You Feel That You Are Losing the Battle

If you have adult children who have been captured by evil influences and destructive behavior, and they keep relapsing back into it once they are set free, refuse to give up and stop praying. Over and over the Bible talks about how God delivered His people from the enemy. God *can deliver* us and He promises to *continue to deliver us,* and that includes your adult children. The apostle Paul said, "We had the sentence of death in ourselves, that we should not trust in ourselves but in God who raises the dead, who delivered us from so great a death, and *does deliver us;* in whom we trust that *He will still deliver us,* you also helping together in prayer for us" (2 Corinthians 1:9–11, emphasis added). God will not stop the deliverance and restoration process as long as we and our adult children are willing to keep praying.

Sometimes it may seem that the more you pray, the worse it gets. But you can't back down. *If the enemy has turned up the intensity, you need to turn up the fervency.* Often the battle becomes more intense the closer you get to victory. Just as a mother forgets about the pain of childbirth the moment she sees her newborn baby, when you are about to give birth to victory you have to push through the pain and keep praying until you see the birth of answered prayer. "Weeping may endure for a night, but joy comes in the morning" (Psalm 30:5). Think about the joy of success that is ahead.

God does not want you to get discouraged, but rather to be a prisoner of hope. Instead of being chained to sadness, fear, hopelessness, or dread, let hope in the Lord feed your faith. Determine to walk by faith and not by sight. Take the dream in your heart that you have for your adult child and declare that the victory you see for him or her has already been won in the name of Jesus.

Pray that God will reveal Himself to your adult children. Even though He will not violate their will, when you pray for them the power of God is invited to penetrate their lives. God has countless ways in which He can penetrate their hearts so that they become more open to His influence.

Above all, do not allow the enemy to make you feel that you are disqualified from powerful intercession for your adult children because of mistakes you may have made in the past. Whatever you neglected to do — or couldn't do because of human frailties, inabilities, limitations, or overwhelming burdens when raising your children — there is a promise that God will more than compensate for that by the flow of His Spirit of grace and power moving into their lives. You have the authority to call upon the Deliverer on behalf of your adult children so that they can find the deliverance they need.

Remember that "all things work together for good to those who love God, to those who are the called according to His purpose" (Romans 8:28). Remember too that the verses before this one are talking about prayer. Things work together for good *if we are praying.* Don't forget that "in all these things we are more than conquerors through Him who loved us" (Romans 8:37).

God is looking for people who love Him so that He can come to their rescue. "The eyes of the LORD run to and fro throughout the whole earth, to show Himself strong on behalf of those whose heart is loyal to Him" (2 Chronicles 16:9). Ask the Lord to show Himself strong on behalf of you and your adult children today.

Pray That God Will Destroy Any Spirit of Rebellion

Too many adult children are suffering because their parents failed to teach and demonstrate that there are serious consequences for wrong actions. We are supposed to have corrected our children, just as God corrects us because He loves us. If we haven't corrected them the way we should have — if we indulged them instead, or if our correction became abusive rather than corrective — we too will pay the consequences when we see the results. "The rod and rebuke give wisdom, but a child left to himself brings shame to his mother" (Proverbs 29:15).

God understands the pain, sorrow, struggle, hurt, disappointment, and frustration we feel as parents. God is the Almighty King of the universe and Creator of all things, but He is still our *heavenly Father.*

He must have surely felt sorrow when we, His children, were rebellious and ungrateful and determined to do things *our* way. As parents, we *grieve* over our children's mistakes or bad choices. We *hurt* when hurtful things happen to them. We are *angered* over their rebellion to the ways of God.

We all make mistakes as parents, so let's get those memories out of our hearts and minds by going before the Lord and asking Him to reveal anything that needs to be put under the cross and submitted to the delivering power of the Holy Spirit. Say, "Lord, show me if I have failed to discipline my children when they were younger and this has encouraged rebelliousness or caused them to not understand the consequences of sin now." If you see places where you have overindulged your child or failed to discipline when you should have, *don't let the enemy win this.* Confess it before God.

King David in the Bible — the one who God said was a man after His own heart — failed as a parent. He did terrible things that went against what he knew to be right. It is said of Adonijah, David's rebellious son, that "his father had not rebuked him at any time" (1 Kings 1:5–6). David did not discipline Adonijah at all, which would have done a great deal to shape him into a decent human being instead of the self-centered brat he became. He rebelled against his father and came to a disastrous end. Children who are not disciplined become self-centered, self-serving, and eventually self-destructive. David didn't do what he needed to do to shape his son into the man of God he should have been, and so Adonijah did what he wanted because he knew no consequences.

The story of Adonijah shows us that the consequences are severe when children are not raised the Lord's way. But God does not want anyone to be destroyed as Adonijah was. He wants them to be repentant instead (2 Peter 3:9).

Young kids who are lovingly disciplined and learn the rules and boundaries grow up to be more secure adults. I'm not talking about beating; I am talking about shaping. Raising a child takes love and discipline, but the rewards are great. "No chastening seems to be joyful for the present, but painful; nevertheless, afterward it yields the peaceable fruit of righteousness to those who have been trained by it" (Hebrews 12:11). The Bible says, "Do not withhold correction from a child" (Proverbs 23:13). It says that our child's destiny is affected by the way we discipline him. And that if we discipline him, we "deliver his soul from hell" (Proverbs 23:14).

In other words, if we don't discipline our children, the devil will.

When we discipline our children, it protects them from the enemy. And our peace is affected as well. "Correct your son, and he will give you rest; yes, he will give delight to your soul" (Proverbs 29:17). Disobedience without any consequences opens the door for a spirit of rebellion. Rebellion causes a person to be influenced and swayed by the enemy. The Bible says we are not to "give place to the devil" (Ephesians 4:27). A rebellious nature indicates that a person has given the enemy a place in their heart. Rebellion evaporates all wisdom and discernment and allows your adult children to open up to a realm that is dark and evil (1 Samuel 15:23). Rebellion is never harmless. It always brings trouble. Pray for a breaking of any rebelliousness in your adult children.

Your prayers can not only keep the enemy from gaining any more ground in their lives now, but they can push him back completely. Just remember that your battle is with the enemy and not with your adult children. And the Holy Spirit in you is more powerful than the enemy's influence in them. There is nothing too hard for God.

"Ah, Lord God! Behold, You have made the heavens and the earth by Your great power and outstretched arm. There is nothing too hard for You" (Jeremiah 32:17).

No matter how far away from God or deep in rebellion our adult children are, God has promised to save them and bring them back from where they have been taken captive. "Do not be dismayed, O Israel! For behold, *I will save you from afar, and your offspring from the land of their captivity*" (Jeremiah 46:27, emphasis added). Every day say, "Thank You, Lord, that You will bring my adult child back from the land of her (his) captivity."

Don't Hesitate to Call for Reinforcements

This chapter is longer than the others because it is dealing with life-and-death issues. If we don't pray about these things for our adult children, the consequences could be dire. I can't begin to describe the urgency I feel about this. That's why if one or more of your adult children are in a serious struggle, don't just pray alone. Join with others. This is the most powerful thing you can do next to fasting and prayer.

Pastor Jack Hayford said this in one of his sermons about the power of praying together: "There's a biblical principle that the multiplying of partnership in prayer multiplies the dimension of impact. It's taken from the Lord, who said that five will chase a hundred, and a hundred will put ten thousand to flight (Leviticus 26:8). It's not a matter of saying God is obligated because of the number, but there is a penetrating power when there's agreement in prayer. Agreeing is like striking notes in harmony. The words 'one accord' convey the idea of people all having the same temperature — the same degree of passion, the same degree of focus (Acts 2:1, 2:46, 4:24, 5:12). This reality calls us to pray together, believing the same way about what is possible."

He went on to explain that we have to "define what we're going to pray about" and also "understand the biblical grounds upon which we're expecting those things to happen." When we do that our prayers become focused. That's one of the reasons I love praying with other people. It forces us to get focused and pray specifically. When the problem you're praying about is serious, call for reinforcements. Don't hesitate to ask for prayer from others. There are many people who would love to pray with you about whatever concerns you have — especially about your adult children.

When the disciples gathered with others

to pray together, there was a powerful manifestation of the Holy Spirit. "When they had prayed, *the place where they were assembled together was shaken;* and they were all filled with the Holy Spirit, and they spoke the word of God with boldness. Now the multitude of those who believed were of one heart and one soul" (Acts 4:31–32, emphasis added).

The power of their prayers was increased, but not just because there were more bodies. There also had to be more faith combined together with focus. That's where the "one accord" part comes in. When people, such as you and I, join together in agreement about an important matter in prayer, things happen.

It also says that "great grace" was upon them all (Acts 4:33).

Grace is the undeserved favor of God upon us. But the "great grace" referred to here is the power of the Holy Spirit working in our lives and being manifest in response to our prayers. When we are praying for our adult children we need not only grace — more favor from God than we deserve — we need *great grace,* which is the power of the Holy Spirit working in our lives and in the lives of our adult children. We need the place where we are to be shaken. Not necessarily the house or the room, but the situations and the condition of the heart.

Zerubbabel, the Old Testament governor of Judah, was responsible for rebuilding God's temple, but he was instructed to not trust in the strength or resources of man to do it. The Lord wanted Zerubbabel to trust in *Him.* God told him it wouldn't be accomplished "by might nor by power, but by My Spirit" (Zechariah 4:6). God went on to say, "Who are you, O great mountain? Before Zerubbabel you shall become a plain! And he shall bring forth the capstone with *shouts of 'Grace, grace to it!'* " (Zechariah 4:7, emphasis added).

When we speak grace to the hindrance or obstacle we are facing — or that our adult child is facing — which is like a mountain to us, it is an act of faith on our part. We are acknowledging that we don't have the power to change things, but God does. And by His Spirit of grace, He will do it.

When you call upon God in prayer, shout "grace" to whatever mountain of opposition opposes you or your adult child. Say, "Lord, in the name of Jesus I speak grace to that situation." And name the opposition that you want to see broken down. Say, for example:

Lord, I speak grace to my daughter's destructive habits.
Lord, I speak grace to my son's problem with drugs.
Lord, I speak grace to my daughter's eating disorder.
Lord, I speak grace to my son's financial problems.

Speak grace to any mountain of opposition your adult child is facing.

Pray That Your Adult Child Will Come Back to the Lord

There is a passage in the Bible where the Lord is speaking through the prophet Jeremiah and talking to a city of people who were being destroyed by their own corruption. God promises to restore them if they will turn back to Him and repent. These were promises not only for the adults, but for their children as well. The Bible says the Lord's mercy is forever (Psalm 89:28). So even though God is speaking to the people of Israel at that time, He gave a promise to them that we can believe applies to those of us who also pray and weep for our adult children who have been carried away captive by the enemy.

This promise says, " 'Refrain your voice

from weeping, and your eyes from tears; for your work shall be rewarded,' says the LORD, 'and they shall come back from the land of the enemy. There is hope in your future,' says the LORD, 'that your children shall come back to their own border' " (Jeremiah 31:16–17).

If you have adult children who have been taken captive by evil influences, read that verse above again and believe that God is speaking those words to you. These verses say to me that our hard work in prayer for our adult children will be rewarded, because they will come back from the land of the enemy to which they have been taken captive.

This is a great promise for parents of adult children who have strayed off the path God has for their lives. You may not know exactly what the path is that God has for them, but you *do* know if the one they are walking on now is not it. This is a message of hope for your adult children too, for no matter how far the enemy has taken them from the life they were meant to live, they will come back from the land of the enemy to their own border.

Remember what I said about the promises of God? They are not an entitlement program. Something is required on our part.

While it's true that we do get to enjoy what we didn't earn, we still have to pray in order to receive it. We can *weep* in *prayer* for our adult children, but we don't have to *weep* in *despair.* We can praise God for His promises to bring our children back to the way they were raised.

If your adult child has strayed away from your family or your religion, there is a breech in your relationship, or she (he) has chosen a lifestyle that is so far from the way you raised her (him) that it puts you in great distress, pray for her (his) return and restoration. This doesn't mean she (he) will move back in with you, so don't become concerned — or get your hopes up, as the case may be. It means that as you pray, God will pull down that great divide, open up communication again, and help you to re-connect.

If your adult child needs to return to her (his) own border, to come back to the ways of the Lord and what she (he) knows is right, God is saying that He sees your tears and hears your prayers. Keep praying for her (him) until she (he) returns from the land of the enemy to live in your realm — which is the kingdom of God on earth. Don't give up and stop praying about this. Give God a chance to work. Remember that

He is dealing with a strong will in your adult child, which He has sovereignly set Himself not to violate.

How many times have we all wept before the Lord while praying for our adult children? Our hearts are broken when we see anything broken in them. The Bible says that "he who continually goes forth weeping, bearing seed for sowing, shall doubtless come again with rejoicing, bringing his sheaves with him" (Psalm 126:6). When we are sowing seeds in prayer and have watered them with our tears of pain and grief, something powerful happens. When you weep with passion in prayer, you will have joy knowing that something great was accomplished in the spirit realm. And you *will* see it manifest in the physical realm as well.

When What You Need to Say Is Hard for Them to Hear

As I said in the introduction to this book, we cannot just sit back and let our adult children do damage to their lives when we see a dangerous situation brewing. We have to say something. My husband and I have both had to do that with each of our adult children. And each time we did it in love, not anger. Showing love at that time was not our natural first reaction, but our very wise pastor told us that this was the only way to respond if we wanted to see good results.

When we went to each adult child — each at separate times for different reasons — we told them that what they were doing was off the path God had for them and it was unacceptable. We told them we were not about to allow something that would be less than what God has for them to continue happening when we had the ability to step in. We assured each one that we loved him or her too much to let them walk over a cliff when we could help them change course.

We also told them we had asked the Lord to reveal to us anything that needed to be brought to light in either of their lives, and it was entirely of the Lord that we were made aware of certain things that were happening. When we confronted them, they were immediately repentant and did a major path adjustment in their lives. In both cases, they had allowed the influence of ungodly people to steer them in the wrong direction.

Before we confronted each of them, we prayed fervently. We wanted to go to them in the Spirit of the Lord and not in the anger of the flesh, because it was important that we see a change of heart and an opening of their eyes to the truth. And, thank

God, we did. We were grateful to see this become a major turning point in each of their lives. I must say that it was miserable for all of us at the time, but so much good came out of it that I know the Lord was in the details.

Don't think that just because your children are adults they don't need any more input from you. They do, whether they ask for it or not. Just pick your moments. Don't nitpick. Give advice sparingly and only when they seem receptive to it. But if you see them about to hit a wall, don't hesitate to step in and help turn things around.

You will have greater authority in your adult children's lives if you submit yourself to Father God's authority in your own life. By authority I don't mean trying to make your adult children do things your way. I mean being able to have credible input into their lives when they need it. We don't want to stop our adult children from being able to think for themselves and make their own decisions. We want to be a support to them in the decisions they make and yet have credible input if they make a terribly wrong one.

If you have to say something that you know will be hard for your adult child to hear, bathe it in prayer first. Pray for the right words and the right timing. Pray for a receptive heart in your adult child.

If you have asked God to get your adult child's attention and set her (him) on the right path, be aware when He is doing exactly that. Sometimes God allows things to happen — or not happen, as the case may be — in order to cause her (him) to rethink her (his) actions. It may be hard to watch, but it will be worth it when you see a breakthrough.

Trust your instincts when it comes to your adult children. This is not a license to be suspicious of them all the time, but you should be suspicious of the enemy at all times. If you sense something is not right with your adult children — or something troubles you in your soul regarding them — trust that instinct! God gives parents special holy antennae that can pick up evil a mile away. Start praying immediately for God to reveal everything and expose any sin so that repentance, deliverance, and healing can begin. You've got the power. The enemy has only lies. Pray that all truth will come to light.

Lord, I pray that You will give (name of adult child) the discernment she (he) needs to understand the clear choice between good and evil, and right and wrong, between what is life giving and life destroying, and between a path into a secure and good future and a dead-end street. I pray that she (he) will not allow the world to shape her (him), but instead she (he) would be shaped by You. I know that the influence of the enemy can come in so subtly as to be nearly unobserved until it's too late. But I pray that with Holy Spirit–given wisdom and discernment she (he) can be prepared for the enemy and anticipate his plans. Help her (him) to "be saved from this perverse generation" (Acts 2:40).

I pray that this worldly culture will not have a hold on her (him). Sever any attachment in her (him) for the evil of the world and free her (him) to be attached only to You. Protect her (him) from every attack of the enemy. Help her (him) to trust in You and Your power and not "give place to the devil" (Ephesians 4:27). I pray that she (he) would seek Your guidance for her (his) life.

Lord, I pray for my adult child that You would be her (his) "hiding place" where she (he) will be preserved from trouble. Surround her (him) "with songs of deliverance" and instruct her (him) in the way she (he) should go. Be her (his) strength in time of trouble and deliver her (him) from the wicked one (Psalm 37:39–40). Thank You, Lord, that You deliver us from our enemies (Psalm 18:48).

Lord, I pray that You would give me wisdom to know how to pray for each of my adult children. Give me courage to confront them when I need to. Help me to wait for the right timing and give me the exact words to say. Open their hearts to hear from me. Wherever they have strayed from Your ways, I pray You would extend Your shepherd's crook and bring them back into the fold.

Where my adult child has been taken captive by evil influences or destructive behavior, I pray that You will set her (him) free. Thank You, Lord, that You have said that my children "shall come back from the land of the enemy" and that there is hope in my future because my "children shall come back to their own border" (Jeremiah 31:16–17).

I realize I don't know everything going on in my adult child's mind, emotions, or life, but You do. Reveal what needs to be revealed. Expose any error of thought so clearly that she (he) is brought to repentance before You. Don't allow her (him) to get away with anything. Wherever she (he) is even toying with something that is an enemy trap for her (his) destruction, I pray You would rescue her (him) out of it. Keep her (him) away from people who intend to do evil or involve her (him) in evil works. Keep her (him) from falling into temptation. Strengthen her (him) to resist all evil influences and avoid all destructive behavior.

Where she (he) has been the victim of evil, I pray that You would heal, restore, and lift her (him) up above it. Bring good out of it. Just as You raised up Joseph to save a nation after evil plots on his life were carried out, I pray You would raise up my daughter (son) to great things in spite of the evil perpetuated on her (his) life. In the meantime, enable her (him) to navigate through this time and find "grace in the wilderness" (Jeremiah 31:2).

Work in her (his) life to bring her (him) into full alignment with Your will so there is no room for the enemy to penetrate Your wall of protection. Keep and protect her (him) from the evil one. Open her (his) eyes to see Your truth, so she (he) will be free of any deception. Smash any false idols in her (his) mind that entice her (him) off the path

You have for her (him). Help her (him) to turn her (his) mind away from evil so she (he) will not be conformed to the world. Help her (him) to be transformed by the renewing of her (his) mind so that she (he) will be in Your perfect will (Romans 12:1–2). I know that You will not violate the will of my adult child, but I invite You to penetrate her (his) life by the power of Your Holy Spirit and cause her (his) heart to be touched by Your presence.

Whenever I feel discouraged, or fear we are losing the battle, I will lift up praise to You, for You are far greater than any evil influence my adult child is facing. I pray by the power of Your Holy Spirit that my adult child will be free of all evil influences and destructive behavior. Expose whatever needs to be revealed to Your penetrating and all-seeing light so deliverance and freedom can come.

In Jesus' name I pray.

Word Power

Trust in the Lord with all your heart, and lean not on your own understanding; in all your ways acknowledge Him, and He shall direct your paths.
Proverbs 3:5–6

For the weapons of our warfare are not carnal but mighty in God for pulling down strongholds.
2 Corinthians 10:4

You who love the Lord, hate evil! He preserves the souls of His saints; He delivers them out of the hand of the wicked. Light is sown for the righteous, and gladness for the upright in heart. Rejoice in the Lord, you righteous, and give thanks at the remembrance of His holy name.
Psalm 97:10–12

The Lord is my rock and my fortress and my deliverer; my God, my strength, in whom I will trust.
Psalm 18:2

"Not by might nor by power, but by

My Spirit," says the LORD of hosts.
ZECHARIAH 4:6

9
Pray That Your Adult Children Will Avoid All Sexual Pollution and Temptation

In the 30-plus years since my first child was born, I have seen major changes on television that are an indication of what has happened to our culture. When my children were young, we seldom had the television on in the daytime. By the time Michael or I turned it on in the evening to watch the news, a sports program, or something special that we were interested in, the kids were in bed. I didn't keep them from watching TV because I was afraid of what they would see, but because I didn't want to numb their brains and hinder their creativity. I wanted them to play outside as much as possible, and when they were inside to be able to think of things to do with their toys, books, games, and ideas.

They were allowed to watch certain videos that I had seen and knew passed the standards of what I felt was beneficial for them. And they did watch special TV shows that were interesting and great fun. But, for the most part, they were in the habit of being busy without the TV and so didn't rely on it. Even when they were staying at a friend's house, I still didn't worry back then about what they would see on TV. It wasn't like how it is today.

Today is different. If I were raising children today, I don't know if I would have a TV within their grasp. Today, even I as an adult cannot just flip channels because there is so much offensive material that is considered normal, run-of-the-mill viewing. There is no way I am going to grieve the Holy Spirit in me and allow my soul to be abused by exposure to such horrible material. Too much of what comes across the television today is polluting *all* of our lives. Our senses can easily become immune to offensive profanity, blatant immorality, constant blaspheming of everything having to do with God, and the exalting of the godless while diminishing the godly.

Our adult children — yours and mine — have been exposed to this kind of influence for years. Our schools have had every possible shred of evidence that God exists, or that Christianity is relevant to their lives, removed from the premises. Nothing of the Ten Commandments is allowed. Prayer has been forbidden. All godly input has been taken away. Yet we've been *inundated* by forces that oppose all that God is and all that He stands for, and we've been encouraged to accept good as evil and evil as good. The voice of the world tries to wipe out the voice of morality. And our adult children have it thrust at them every day in some way.

Above all of this, the pervasive evil of promiscuity, perversion, and casual sex brings confusion into their lives. Perversion is promoted as not only normal, but desirable. Evil has gone out to our kids and adult children and targeted them. Promiscuity means being sexually active now. It implies that if you are not active, or you are a virgin, you're not normal. Our children are being led to believe that promiscuity, or having sex before marriage, is not only good but expected, like a rite of passage. It is promoted as something to be sought after. Sex *outside* of marriage is exalted and presented as being better than sex inside of a marriage. Casual attitudes for immorality have become the plague that infects everyone. We have been inoculated and are now desensitized to its dangers. And I'm not talking about anything more than turning on the TV. Even commercials with sexual or suggestive images can pollute our minds.

In order for our adult children to live successfully in every aspect of their lives, sexual purity is vital. It affects the very center of who they are. It affects their most important relationship in marriage. When they live with sexual pollution in their lives, it affects every part of them. Their relationships become weak, and they lose a sense of their true purpose and identity.

Don't think for a moment that because you or your adult children have never viewed anything even bordering on pornography that your minds have not been polluted in some way. The spirit behind all this — the spirit of lust — is everywhere. Your adult children see sexual images on billboards as they drive down the street. It is a click away on their computer screens as they sit at their desks at home. They see it in regular or normal magazines. They see it in popular films — even in what is supposed to be a decent film. They see it in music videos, and they hear it in the lyrics of certain songs. Sex has become an idol that our culture worships, and our adult children are being enticed to think about it far too much.

What any of us see — even by accident — affects us more than we realize. Images can play over and over in our minds that make us feel a myriad of feelings such as shock, lust, guilt, disgust, or annoyance. These images force our minds to go where we don't want them to go, even if only for a moment. We then have to waste valuable time dealing with those thoughts and feelings. We have to ask God to cleanse our mind of these things so that it doesn't infect good judgment. God tells us over and over in His Word that we are to run away from evil things and not look at them. However, evil is pushed in our faces when we least expect it. And especially our adult children, because many of them haven't known life without it.

What all this means is that we have to pray passionately and fervently for our adult children in order to see God break the power of darkness surrounding their lives.

TEN WAYS TO PRAY FOR YOUR ADULT CHILDREN TO RESIST SEXUAL POLLUTION

1. *Pray that your adult children will have a fresh outpouring of the Holy Spirit upon them.* This will cause them to see with new eyes. When they can see things from God's perspective

and are enabled by the power of the Holy Spirit, they can better resist any attack of sexual pollution by a spirit of lust upon them. "To be carnally minded is death, but to be spiritually minded is life and peace" (Romans 8:6).

2. *Pray that your adult children will have a renewed heart for God, His Word, and His ways.* Being drawn toward the things of God will draw them away from anything that is opposed to God. Having a heart for God's ways and His Word will cause them to be uncomfortable with sexual images or actions that violate or compromise God's ways. "The righteousness of the upright will deliver them, but the unfaithful will be caught by their lust" (Proverbs 11:6).
3. *Pray that your adult children will have wisdom, discernment, and revelation.* They need great wisdom to know how to avoid sexual pollution. They need clear discernment in order to clearly see what is and what isn't sexual pollution. And they need revelation from God about how to protect themselves and live in pu-

rity. "When wisdom enters your heart, and knowledge is pleasant to your soul, discretion will preserve you; understanding will keep you, to deliver you from the way of evil, from the man who speaks perverse things" (Proverbs 2:10–12).

4. *Pray that your adult children will find freedom, restoration, and wholeness.* Pray that they will be free from anything that draws them toward whatever is sexually polluting. Pray that they will be delivered from anything that has a hold on them, such as sexual images in their mind that have come through any form of media. Pray that they will find restoration from any brokenness or sexual failure in their past so that they can have the renewed purity and wholeness God has for them. "Therefore submit to God. Resist the devil and he will flee from you" (James 4:7).
5. *Pray that your adult children will not let their eyes look at worthless things.* Pray that they will refuse to even glance at something that is offensive to God and adds nothing of value for their lives. "Turn away my eyes

from looking at worthless things, and revive me in Your way. Establish Your word to Your servant, who is devoted to fearing You" (Psalm 119:37–38).

6. *Pray that your adult children will not get their focus off of the path and purpose God has for them.* It is important to always understand their purpose so that they refuse to violate that in any way. "Let your eyes look straight ahead, and your eyelids look right before you" (Proverbs 4:25).
7. *Pray that your adult children will recognize the power of lust to destroy their souls.* Because "everyone is doing it" doesn't make it okay for them. God expects more than that. They have to resist the enemy in this war for their souls. "Beloved, I beg you as sojourners and pilgrims, abstain from fleshly lusts which war against the soul" (1 Peter 2:11).
8. *Pray that your adult children will see lust in any form as being against God's will.* Understanding the will of God for their lives needs to be their priority. "That he no longer should live the rest of his time in

the flesh for the lusts of men, but for the will of God" (1 Peter 4:2).

9. *Pray that your adult children will live in the Spirit of God and not in the lust of the flesh.* They need to clearly understand what is of the Holy Spirit and what are fleshly desires that do not glorify God. "I say then: Walk in the Spirit, and you shall not fulfill the lust of the flesh" (Galatians 5:16).
10. *Pray that your adult children will run to the Lord and the truth of His Word whenever they are tempted to be drawn into any kind of sexual pollution.* The consequences of doing otherwise are too serious to consider. It is a matter of life and death in so many ways. "Before I was afflicted I went astray, but now I keep Your word" (Psalm 119:67).

If There Is Already a Problem

If you know or suspect your adult child has a problem, such as an immoral lifestyle or an interest in pornography or whatever else, fast and pray for him (her). Even a single 18- to 24-hour fast, where you drink only water and pray to God about this every time you feel hungry, can bring miraculous breakthrough. God says that the purpose of fasting is *"to loose the bonds of wickedness, to undo the heavy burdens, to let the oppressed go free"* and to *"break every yoke"* (Isaiah 58:6, emphasis added). All this is reason enough to fast and pray right there. To see these things happen for your adult child would be glorious. And who will do this on his (her) behalf if *you* don't do it? Your adult child needs your help to get free.

The devil knows your adult child's weakness and will attack him (her) in that area. If a spirit of lust is trying to control your adult child's mind, it will destroy his (her) soul as well, and possibly his (her) life. Even watching one moment of sexually polluting images can stay in his (her) mind for as long as the enemy is allowed to repeatedly flash them back. "By means of a harlot a man is reduced to a crust of bread; and an adulteress will prey upon his precious life. Can a man take fire to his bosom, and his clothes not be burned?" (Proverbs 6:26–27). Sexual pollution will begin to destroy not only who he (she) is, but who he (she) *can* be.

Every time we commit a sin an evil spirit is waiting to establish a stronghold in our lives. When we repeatedly give place to that sin, the stronghold becomes more entrenched. Unrepented sin invites evil into our lives, keeping us from all God has for us. God will allow us to be miserable until we give up the sin in favor of living *His* way.

Jesus said, "If anyone desires to come after Me, let him deny himself, and take up his cross, and follow Me" (Matthew 16:24). Pray that your adult child will deny himself (herself) any access to sexual pollution and will do whatever necessary to avoid anything that is a temptation. The Bible says we "should repent, turn to God, and do works befitting repentance" (Acts 26:20). Pray that he (she) will repent and stop doing what he (she) has been doing and start living God's way.

A person struggling in this area cannot face it alone (Ecclesiastes 4:12). Sexual pollution is a powerful and pervasive opposition. If this is a serious problem with your adult child, find others you can trust to pray with you about it.

God seeks people who will stand in the gap and pray where there is sin. In the book of Ezekiel God said, "I sought for a man among them who would make a wall, and stand in the gap before Me on behalf of the land, that I should not destroy it; but I found no one" (Ezekiel 22:30). The gap He is talking about is between God and man, and the person who stands in the gap is the one who prays. A gap was also a place in the protective wall around a field or a city that had been broken down and needed repair. God only needed one person to pray, and He couldn't find even one.

Someone who comes before God on behalf of another is an intercessor. As an intercessor for our adult children, we can stand in that gap when the protective wall around them has been broken down because of a violation of God's laws. Our prayers can help to repair the breech in that wall of protection.

God warned of all the terrible things that would happen because the people had gone after the world's idols and had become defiled by them. He said, "I will do these things to you because you have gone as a harlot after the Gentiles, because you have become defiled by their idols" (Ezekiel 23:30). Pray that your adult children don't become defiled by the world's idols. Your prayers can help strengthen them enough to resist all temptation. If they have already succumbed, they need your prayers to break the power those idols have in their lives.

In a prayer for relief from Israel's oppressors, a psalmist asked God not to forget them, but instead to remember His covenant with them. He prayed, "Have respect to the covenant; for the dark places of the earth are full of the haunts of cruelty" (Psalm 74:20). That is true today. The dark places of our world are full of the haunts of cruelty. And often these places start with sexual pollution and perversion. Seeds that grow into a seemingly unstoppable force. Some of the "haunts of cruelty" in dark places on the earth are pornography, forced prostitution, and especially child pornography and sexual abuse. There are many others, but these are among the worst. And they all began as a thought, action, or glance at a sexually polluting image.

We want our adult children to have clear-eyed freedom in the Lord. We want it to be said of them that they "looked to Him and were radiant, and their faces were not ashamed" (Psalm 34:5). We must pray for their protection and their liberation because they are being inundated with sexual pollution.

PRAYER POWER

Lord, I pray for (name of adult child) to be free of all sexual pollution. Wherever he (she) has seen things that have compromised his (her) sexual purity, I pray You would cleanse his (her) mind of it and take it out of his (her) heart. If he (she) has willingly become involved in anything that violates Your standards for purity, I pray that You would convict his (her) conscience about it and bring him (her) to repentance before You. Help him (her) to willingly turn away from every idol and abominable thing (Ezekiel 14:6). Break the power of any spirit of lust that attempts to bring death to his (her) soul (Ezekiel 18:31–32).

Help him (her) to flee sexual pollution — to turn away from it, not look at it, and not be drawn into it — and to refuse to be defiled by the world's idols (Ezekiel 23:30). Give him (her) the conviction to change the channel; shut down the website; throw out the magazine, DVD, or CD; or walk out of the theater (Proverbs 27:12). Give him (her) understanding that any deviation from the path You have for him (her) — even if it is only occurring in the mind — will be a trap to fall into and a snare for his (her) soul.

Enable him (her) to stand on the solid ground of purity in Your sight. Help him (her) to see that even unintended disobedience to Your ways will require a cleansing on his (her) part. Help him (her) to hide Your Word in his (her) heart so that he (she) will not sin against You (Psalm 119:9–11). I pray that he (she) will be protected by discretion and attracted to the knowledge and understanding that will deliver him (her) from evil (Proverbs 2:10–12).

Where he (she) has allowed any ungodly desires, I pray You would set him (her) free. Put desire in his (her) heart to please You by walking in the Spirit and not the flesh (Romans 8:8). Help him (her) to know that You are his (her) refuge and he (she) can turn to You anytime temptation is presenting itself (Psalm 141:8). Help him (her) to understand the greatness of Your power to set him (her) free. Turn his (her) eyes away from worthless things (Psalm 119:37). Give him (her) the ability to truly ponder everything he (she) does and every step taken so that he (she) will not walk in the path of evil (Proverbs 4:26–27).

Wherever there has been any moral failure on his (her) part, give him (her) a heart of repentance so that he (she) can come before You and be cleansed of all the effects and consequences of it. I pray that he (she) will never be seduced down a path that leads to destruction. Open his (her) eyes to every lie presenting itself as truth. Enable him (her) to resist all temptation. Give him (her) the "spirit of wisdom and revelation" so that he (she) will understand the purpose for which he (she) was created and not want to violate it (Ephesians 1:17–18).

Lord, You have said that sin happens just by looking at something bad (Matthew 5:28). But you gave us a way to get rid of the propensity for it (Matthew 5:29). I pray that my adult child will get rid of anything in his (her) life that causes him (her) to compromise the purity of soul that You want. Don't let the light in his (her) eyes die because of seeing sexual pollution. Help him (her) to look to You instead (Psalm 123:1). Enable him (her) to say as David did, "I will set nothing wicked before my eyes" (Psalm 101:3).

I pray for a breaking down of the idols of sexual promiscuity, pornography, perversion, sensuality, and immorality in the media, in our land, in our homes, and in our lives. I pray especially that my adult children will not be tempted, trapped, swayed, or polluted by any of it.

In Jesus' name I pray.

For all that is in the world — the lust of the flesh, the lust of the eyes, and the pride of life — is not of the Father but is of the world.
1 JOHN 2:16

Repent, turn away from your idols, and turn your faces away from all your abominations.
EZEKIEL 14:6

Who may ascend into the hill of the LORD? Or who may stand in His holy place? He who has clean hands and a pure heart, who has not lifted up his soul to an idol, nor sworn deceitfully. He shall receive blessing from the Lord, and righteousness from the God of his salvation.
PSALM 24:3–5

A prudent man foresees evil and hides himself; the simple pass on and are punished.
PROVERBS 27:12

Confess your trespasses to one another, and pray for one another, that you may be healed. The effective, fervent prayer

of a righteous man avails much.
JAMES 5:16

10
Pray That Your Adult Children Will Experience Good Health and God's Healing

My children were raised with healthy habits. They knew how to eat right, exercise, and get enough sleep. And they were not sick much when they were young. In fact, they each received awards for perfect attendance when they were in grade school. But after they were out on their own, they developed amnesia. They "forgot" most of what they learned. They ate the way they wanted to, didn't exercise, and had terrible sleep habits, all without any regard for the consequences.

After they had grown up and left our home, I would see them making bad choices regarding their body care. They were eating way too much junk — from my son having diet colas for breakfast followed by many more throughout the day, for example, to my daughter never seeing anything made with white flour that she didn't like or eat. They were eating other bad things as well, which didn't help, but I cite these two examples because they have special significance.

Besides eating junk and not exercising, they also kept terrible hours and went too often without enough good sleep. Because I know what those kinds of things do to the body, I was very concerned. I spoke to them about it over and over, but my words fell on deaf ears. It wasn't that they were deliberately rebelling against what I was saying; they just felt they had plenty of time to mend their ways. They later explained such careless actions by saying that because they had been healthy and well nearly all of their early years, they took their good health for granted and assumed it would always be there for them.

Knowing they were going to have to learn some hard lessons, I prayed for them to wake up and understand what they were doing to themselves before something terrible happened. "Lord, help them to understand the truth about their bodies being Your temple and teach them to care for it. Get their attention before they destroy their health." It wasn't until each of them had disturbing and uncomfortable symptoms that they radically changed their ways.

That day came for both of them when

they were in their twenties, and they each began to have serious problems with their health. (Different symptoms and different times for each of them.) As certain symptoms in each one of them became progressively noticeable, I had my prayer group pray with me that they would each have an awakening before it was too late.

My daughter was getting sicker by the day, manifesting symptoms in nearly every part of her body, but the doctors could not find what was wrong with her. She was seriously losing weight, which horrified her because she felt unattractive being so thin. It seemed as though an all-out attack was being waged upon her body, and it was becoming unbearable. To make a very long story short, after seeing a number of different specialists, God led us to one particular doctor who tested her for many things and found out she is gluten intolerant. Anything that has wheat — or any other grain that contains gluten, which is just about every grain except rice and corn — was basically destroying her body.

Her doctor put Amanda on a strict gluten-free diet and she began to improve. Another specialist found other foods she was allergic to and other imbalances in her system as well, which we now know are more common to those who are gluten intolerant. After getting off these foods and taking natural supplements under the advice of these specialists, her life turned completely around. She has become strong and vibrant and has new life in her.

God answered our prayers, but we are still praying for her to be completely healed of all these allergies. They make her life very difficult, especially when she has to travel. God is the God of the impossible, and we are praying for and believing that one day God will do what is humanly impossible and set her free from this burden. Whether He does or not is in His hands. For now, Amanda has learned a new way of eating, and she is extremely diligent to see that she never takes chances in any way with her health.

My son's symptoms were just as bad as my daughter's and every bit as frightening. Christopher started having serious attacks of dizziness and numbness on one side of his body that made him feel as if he were having a stroke or heart attack. He was in the doctor's office and the emergency room a number of times, and on each occasion they told him it must be stress related because they could not find anything wrong with him on any of the tests they had taken.

As a result, it was recommended that he go to a psychiatrist, who could prescribe something to relieve these symptoms of stress. When he went to the psychiatrist, the doctor said it couldn't be stress because stress symptoms don't happen on just one side of the body.

So the psychiatrist sent him to a neurologist, who took more tests and told him it appeared from his symptoms and from the tests that he had either multiple sclerosis or else he'd had mini strokes. He told him to come back to the hospital the following week to take another major, expensive test that would reveal for certain if it was either of those ailments.

My son and I both separately looked up multiple sclerosis in our big medical books and were frightened to see that he had every symptom of it. In fact, it sounded as though this was exactly what he had, and we were very concerned. All this was what I had been praying for years would *not* happen. To think of my healthy son having an incapacitating disease all because he had been negligent with his health was heartbreaking to me. What an unnecessary loss. Christopher was extremely worried as well.

I called on my prayer group to pray, and my husband and I and our son and daughter prayed fervently every day and night that this would not be a life sentence for him. But if it was what we feared, we prayed that God would bring healing to his body.

Early one morning when I was in prayer about this, I reminded God that I had prayed every day for my son's health from the time he was born and even before. And I prayed fervently every day for him as an adult to be healthy and stop abusing his body. Then God brought the Scripture alive to my heart that said the servants of the Lord would not bring forth children for trouble — and that we who serve God would be blessed and so would our children (Isaiah 65:23). My son was dedicated to the Lord from the time he was born, and he was prayed for every day of his life. I felt God was saying that we were to believe that he was not brought forth for trouble. I shared that with my son and daughter and husband, and we all prayed, "Thank You, Lord, that Christopher was not brought forth for trouble."

When we finally got the results of the MRI days later, we found out it was not multiple sclerosis after all, nor was it a stroke. Ultimately, we discovered that he is very allergic to a synthetic sweetener found in the particular diet colas and "health bars" he had been consuming every day. We sent him to the same specialist we had sent our daughter to and found that he is allergic to a number of other things as well. His body had specific imbalances that were all treated with supplements, proper diet, and allergy treatments. He is a new person. He eats amazingly well. He has stamina, he looks strong and fit, and he is healthy. And now both of my adult children exercise five days a week at a gym and often with a personal trainer.

The outcomes of these two stories are a miracle to all of us, because there were times with each of them when their struggle seemed so great and there was no sign of breakthrough. But when we started to get discouraged, we prayed all the more. We were persistent in prayer because we had the faith and determination to not give up until we saw the healing and help we needed.

Both my son and daughter have seen a major turnaround in their lives. They each feel that they have been given new life and they want to help others feel well too. As a result, my son is now getting his master's degree in holistic nutrition, while working in his career as a record producer and songwriter. He saw what an amazing transformation can happen in our bodies when we treat them right. My daughter is studying different forms of physical therapy for the same reason. She knows the healing power of touch therapy and wants to help others to be free of pain and find greater health and healing for themselves.

I never dreamed I would see either of my adult children doing any of these things. And I certainly never thought I would see the day when they would be giving me health advice, which they both do now on a regular basis.

What a difference from a few years ago when I was so concerned about both of them that I prayed day and night for their health. God not only healed them, but He also turned their lives completely around.

If you have ever looked at your adult children's health habits and felt concern, know that your prayers for their awakening do not fall on deaf ears with God. He will hear you and answer. Just don't stop praying until you see results.

Learning to Maintain Good Health

I'm treating *health care* and *healing* in this chapter as two different issues. *Health care* is something *we do* to protect our body. We treat it right and with care. *Healing* is something we pray for and the *Lord does* in response to our prayers.

God expects us to be good stewards over what He gives us, including our bodies. He wants us to care for them and not abuse them in any way. It's sad but true that we are much more diligent about taking care of our health *after* we've lost it. We can be horribly negligent of our bodies when we think we can get away with it. And we have a tendency to push our health as far as we can. We all have endless excuses for why we don't take better care of ourselves. "I'm too busy." "I'm not motivated." "It's too much trouble." "I don't know what to do." "I'm not worth it." "I don't really need it." We find it hard to be disciplined, or we just plain don't want to do it.

Ask God to show your adult children what to do in order to maintain good health. Ask Him to teach them what to eat, how to exercise, and what to do or not do in order to get good, rejuvenating sleep. Ask God to give them *wisdom* to make right choices for good health, *discernment* to know what is good for them and what is bad, and *revelation* about what is right for their particular body.

Knowing Jesus as Their Healer

Jesus is our Healer, and being certain of that is a *must.* God knows we can't do everything perfectly, and that's why He sent Jesus to not only save us, forgive us, and deliver us from the enemy, but also to heal us.

In addition to praying for our adult children to have good health habits, we must also pray that they come to know Jesus as their Healer. There will be times when they will get sick or injured, and they must know how to pray for healing in Jesus' name. When the care of their health fails, they need the power of God to make them well. He may do that through the help of doctors, by revealing something to them that they need to know and do, or by a sovereign work of His grace.

After Jesus was crucified, resurrected, and had ascended into heaven, God poured out His Spirit upon Jesus' disciples. Peter, then being filled with the Holy Spirit, went with John to the temple, where he saw a man who had been lame from birth sitting at the gate asking for money. Peter said to the man these now-famous words, "Silver and gold I do not have, but what I do have I give to you: *In the name of Jesus Christ of Nazareth, rise up and walk*" (Acts 3:6, emphasis added). Then Peter "took him by the right hand and lifted him up, and immediately his feet and ankle bones received strength" (Acts 3:7). He leaped up, walked, and praised God, and the people who saw him walking "were filled with wonder and amazement at what had happened to him" (Acts 3:10).

When Peter saw the people's response, he said, "Why look so intently at us, as though by our own power or godliness we had made this man walk?" (Acts 3:12). He explained that it was God, glorifying His Son, Jesus, whom He had raised from the dead. Then came the most important part of this story. Peter said, "And His name, *through faith in His name,* has made this man strong, whom you see and know. Yes, *the faith which comes through Him has given him this perfect soundness* in the presence of you all" (Acts 3:16, emphasis added).

Peter is saying that it wasn't by any special powers of his own that this man was healed, but by the power of the name of Jesus. *Faith* in Jesus' name *ignites* the power that heals, and *prayer directs* the power to bring us healing.

This is the first miracle recorded as being performed by one of Jesus' disciples. And in the telling of what happened, we can see clearly how we are to pray. Peter commanded healing for the lame man, but he prayed in the name of *Jesus Christ of Nazareth.* By speaking the full name of Jesus, His title, and where He came from, there was no mistaking whom he was talking about. Peter was saying that healing came through *this Jesus* and by no other means. If this account of healing was important enough to be included in the Bible, it is important enough for us to remember it when we are praying for our adult children, as well as ourselves or anyone else.

When we confess that Jesus Christ is Lord, and He has given us power and authority in His name to command sickness and disease to go, we are claiming our authority over all sickness or disease or any power of hell that comes against us. There is power in the name of Jesus because of what He accomplished on the cross. It is not the power of our faith, as if *we* accomplish it. Healing happens because we put our faith in Jesus' name. The power is in His name.

The enemy of our soul always wants to convince us that we are hopeless in our infirmities and there is no way God is going to heal us or our adult children. He also knows that hopelessness weakens us as much as disease. In fact, I'm sure that too much hopelessness contributes to the advancement of some diseases. So we have to pray for ever-increasing faith to believe that what the Bible says is true, and what Jesus says is true. We have to pray that the hope in us, because of what Jesus has accomplished on our behalf, will never fail or weaken.

The man who was lame from birth was healed because of the power of Jesus' name. Did Jesus' name have power only when Peter prayed in that name? Or does the name of Jesus Christ have power when anyone who believes prays in that name? I believe that if God is the same yesterday, today, and forever, and what Jesus accomplished on the cross was accomplished for all time and all people, then the power of His name is for us who believe now. It wasn't only for Peter and John in that moment.

The Bible is too often restricted by some people saying, "This part was only for the disciples, that part was only for the Corinthians, this part is only for the Israelites," and on and on until the entire Bible is explained away and it becomes merely a history book, and an oftentimes difficult one to understand. Don't let men take away what God has given you in His Word. Don't let them tell you God is silent and He doesn't speak to people anymore. Or that He doesn't heal people anymore. Or that He doesn't do miracles anymore. Either He is the same yesterday, today, and forever, or He isn't. The Bible tells us who God *is,* not who He *was.* Don't let anyone steal your healing by undermining your faith in the name of Jesus and His ability to heal. He was the Healer. He *is* the Healer. He will *always be* the Healer.

Five Ways to Pray for Health and Healing for Your Adult Children

1. *Pray that your adult children will understand how important their body is to the Lord.* "Do you not know that your body is the temple of the Holy Spirit who is in you, whom you have from God, and you are not your own? For you were bought at a price; therefore glorify God in your body and in your spirit, which are God's" (1 Corinthians 6:19–20).
2. *Pray that your adult children will live God's way.* "In the way of righteousness is life, and in its pathway there is no death" (Proverbs 12:28).

3. *Pray that your adult children will know God as their Healer.* "I am the LORD who heals you" (Exodus 15:26).
4. *Pray that your adult children will have strong faith to pray for healing.* "And the prayer of faith will save the sick, and the Lord will raise him up. And if he has committed sins, he will be forgiven" (James 5:15).
5. *Pray that your adult children will be healed by God.* " 'For I will restore health to you and heal you of your wounds,' says the LORD" (Jeremiah 30:17).

Pray for Boldness to Speak God's Word About Healing

After Peter and John were released from prison and went to their companions to tell them what happened, they prayed together saying, " 'Lord, You are God, who made heaven and earth and the sea, and all that is in them . . . Now, Lord, look on their threats, and grant to Your servants that with all boldness they may speak Your word by *stretching out Your hand to heal,* and that signs and wonders may be done through the name of Your holy Servant Jesus.' And when they had prayed, the place where they were assembled together was shaken; and they were all filled with the Holy Spirit, and they spoke the word of God with boldness" (Acts 4:24,29–31, emphasis added).

This powerful shaking happened because they prayed together in unity, with the same conviction, faith, and intent. They asked God to enable them to *speak His Word with boldness.* They asked Him *to stretch out His hand and heal* and *do signs and wonders in the name of Jesus.* And God answered that prayer in a powerful and mighty way. We too can ask God to help us speak His Word with boldness, especially the verses from Scripture pertaining to healing. You will find some of those Scriptures under the "Word Power" on the last page of this chapter. Ask God to enable you to speak God's Word boldly today. Doing so increases your faith to believe that God can and will heal you in the name of Jesus.

When Facing Serious Health Threats

If your adult child is facing a serious threat to his or her health, pray with other people of faith who believe as you do that Jesus is the Healer and that prayer in His name is powerful enough to bring healing. Speak God's Word in faith, and praise God for His great power that moves on our behalf.

Ask God to show you if there is any

disobedience to His ways happening in your adult child. When Moses brought the people of Israel out of Egypt, across the Red Sea, and into the wilderness, he cried out to God for help to find water to drink. The Lord showed him how to purify polluted water and then told him that if they would keep the Lord's commands and do what He was telling them to do, He would protect them from disease and heal them (Exodus 15:26).

God made it clear that we have to live His way if we expect to have health and healing. Too often we have stressed out our bodies, lived without peace or joy, eaten carelessly and poorly, and gone without sleep or exercise. Or we have given place to sin that opens the door for infirmity or disease. Ask God to show you the truth about your adult children.

There are times when the healing will occur in heaven, and that is not the answer we were praying for or wanted to hear. If that happens to one of your children, pray for God's healing in your heart and restoration for your soul. No one should ever have to bury their child — not even their adult child. Surely there is no greater pain, and it is only by God's grace and love that we even live through it. But the time of death for anyone is entirely in the Lord's hands. Your hope is that you will see your child again in heaven.

If you know your deceased child had received the Lord, then you know she (he) is with the Lord now. If you don't know whether she (he) received the Lord before death, then you don't know that she (he) *didn't,* either. You never know if in that moment before someone dies, the Lord appears to him or her and there is a full recognition and receiving of Jesus as Savior. God is the only one who knows that. Have peace in knowing that it is God's will that none perish apart from Him. Knowing the love and goodness of God as I do, I don't doubt that He has redeemed many before death that we don't even know about. With the Lord, there is always hope to see your children again — no matter what age they were when they left this world.

I believe it is always the will of God to heal. Why would Jesus come as our Healer if He didn't want to heal us? Why is so much said in the Bible about healing us? As to why not everyone is healed who asks for it, only God knows. Ask Him to show you how to proclaim His promises of healing and put great faith in the healing power of the name of Jesus. No matter what the doctor's report is, do not stop praying for total healing. Pray every day that your adult children will live a long and healthy life.

PRAYER POWER

Lord, I pray that (name of adult child) will enjoy good health and a long life. Give her (him) the wisdom and knowledge necessary to recognize that her (his) body is the temple of Your Holy Spirit and that it should be cared for and nurtured and not disregarded or mistreated. Help her (him) to value good health as a gift from You to be protected and not squandered on foolish or careless living. Instill in her (his) heart not to take good health for granted.

Teach her (him) how to make wise choices and to reject anything that undermines good health. Reveal any truth that needs to be seen, and give her (him) understanding. Teach her (him) to be disciplined in the way of eating and exercising and getting proper rest. Help her (him) to bring her (his) body into submission (1 Corinthians 9:27). Give her (him) wisdom and discernment about what to do and what not to do — about what is good and what is bad. Help her (him) to recognize any place where she (he) has given place to careless health care habits that are destroying her (his) life. Help her (him) to value her (his) body enough to take care of it, and teach her (him) the right way to live.

I pray that she (he) will learn to pray in

power for her (his) healing. Raise up in her (him) great faith in the name of Jesus. Give her (him) the understanding to claim the healing that was achieved at the cross. Any place in her (his) body where there is sickness, disease, infirmity, or injury, I pray You would touch her (him) and bring complete healing. Help her (him) to not give up praying until she (he) sees the total healing You have for her (him). Whether her (his) healing is instantaneous or it manifests in a gradual recuperation, I thank You in advance for the miracle of healing You will do in her (his) body. Enable her (him) to see that it is You who have healed and not human power.

Guide all doctors who see and treat her (him). Enable them to make the correct diagnosis and to know exactly what to do. Where healing seems to be a long time in coming, help us to not lose heart or hope, but to instead increase the fervency and frequency of our prayers.

Whenever she (he) is sick, I pray You would be her (his) Healer. I pray for healing for (name of adult child) and I specifically pray for the healing of (name area of body that needs healing). Restore health to her (him) and heal all wounds (Jeremiah 30:17). Give her (him) the knowledge and faith to say, "Oh Lord my God, I cried out to You, and You healed me" (Psalm 30:2). I know that when *You* heal us, we are truly healed (Jeremiah 17:14).

Help her (him) to be a good steward of her (his) body and not take good health for granted. Teach her (him) to understand that she (he) should present her (his) body as a living sacrifice, holy and acceptable to You (Romans 12:1). Enable her (him) to understand the idea of glorifying You in the care of her (his) body, because it is Your dwelling place.

In Jesus' name I pray.

Word Power

Bless the LORD, O my soul, and forget not all His benefits: who forgives all your iniquities, who heals all your diseases, who redeems your life from destruction, who crowns you with loving-kindness and tender mercies.
Psalm 103:2–4

Heal me, O LORD, and I shall be healed; save me, and I shall be saved, for You are my praise.
Jeremiah 17:14

If you diligently heed the voice of the LORD your God and do what is right in His sight, give ear to His commandments and keep all His statutes, I will put none of the diseases on you which I have brought on the Egyptians. For I am the Lord who heals you.
Exodus 15:26

But He was wounded for our transgressions, He was bruised for our iniquities; the chastisement for our peace was upon Him, and by His stripes we are healed.
Isaiah 53:5

But to you who fear My name The Sun of Righteousness shall arise with healing in His wings; and you shall go out and grow fat like stall-fed calves.
MALACHI 4:2

11
Pray That Your Adult Children Will Enjoy a Successful Marriage and Raise Godly Children

One of the most important things on our mind as a parent — and one of the greatest desires of our heart for our adult children — is that they will make the right choice when it comes to choosing their lifelong mate. The last thing we want to see happen is a divorce in their future. Although it is not entirely the end of the world if they divorce, and people do recover and go on to live good lives, it is never the desired outcome, and we would rather they get it right the first time. That's why we have to pray fervently for our adult children to have wisdom about this crucial decision. We all know how easy it is to *think* we have met the right person, and it turns out that we were wrong.

Sometimes divorce is inevitable, such as when a person ends up married to someone who is abusive, irresponsible, immoral, unbearable, dangerous, or hopelessly bound by evil influences. If your adult child has already made a mistake like that and it has ended in divorce, you can pray that there will be no divorce in his or her future. You can pray today that the spirit of divorce will not have any part in his or her life from now on.

Pray That Your Adult Child Will Marry a Believer

The first and most important concern for a parent when praying about who their adult child will marry, is that it be someone who is a godly believer in the Lord. There are certain things you can and should ask of your adult children. This is one of them. It's not just something for a parent to nag about, or a way to try and control their lives, but you can make it clear that your greatest desire for them is to marry believers, because it is God's perfect will for them.

A believer is someone with whom your adult child can build a good, solid life on a firm foundation in the ways of God. The thought of your son or daughter marrying a person who is not a believer in God or a follower of God's ways is sad. Marriage is hard enough without being unequally yoked and unable to establish a firm foundation in the Lord.

However, if your adult child has already married someone who is not a believer, take comfort in knowing that it is God's will to answer prayers for salvation. You can pray that God will touch your son-in-law or daughter-in-law with His love and truth and bring him or her into the kingdom. Ask God to use you and other believers to come alongside your adult child's husband or wife in order to become channels of that love.

Two women who have been very close to me in my life are married to unbelieving husbands, and those men are two of the most godly people I have ever known. They are better Christians than many of us who actually are. They already have the whole Christian lifestyle down; now it's a matter of them acknowledging in their heart that Jesus is Lord. They know how to live God's way without knowing God. But they need that relationship with Jesus, and the fullness of the Holy Spirit in them, in order to have an eternal future with the Lord and greater blessings now. We never stop praying for that and believing God will break through their unbelief.

In the Bible, Isaac and Rebekah were very upset when their 40-year-old son Esau married into a godless society far outside of his family's faith and culture, and he had multiple wives who were unbelievers (Genesis 26:34). Specifically, it says of his wives that "they were a grief of mind to Isaac and Rebekah" (Genesis 26:35). Esau knew that this displeased his parents, but he married them anyway. "Esau saw that the daughters of Canaan did not please his father Isaac" (Genesis 28:8).

Rebekah told her husband that she couldn't bear her life because of what Esau did, and if her other son — Esau's twin brother, Jacob — were to do the same thing, then she felt her life would not be worth living. "Rebekah said to Isaac, 'I am weary of my life because of the daughters of Heth; if Jacob takes a wife of the daughters of Heth, like these who are the daughters of the land, what good will my life be to me?' " (Genesis 27:46).

So Rebekah encouraged Jacob to go away to her family's land and find a wife for himself who would be a blessing to her and Isaac. Isaac told Jacob, "You shall not take a wife from the daughters of Canaan" (Genesis 28:1). In other words, Isaac told Jacob not to take an unbeliever for his wife, but to go to his family in another land and take a wife from there. And being an obedient son, that is what he did. In doing so, he found his true love and the greatest blessing in life in his wife Rachel. She eventually became the mother of Joseph, who became one of the greatest leaders in all of Israel's history, because he saved his people from certain destruction. Jacob was also tricked into taking another wife — Rachel's sister, Leah — but that is another story. The point is, the entire 12 tribes of Israel were fathered by Jacob. None came from Esau.

Here were two sons, *raised by the same godly parents,* and one behaved foolishly and the other wisely. One obeyed his parents, and the other did not. One carried out the promise in his family's line, and the other didn't. One had his mind on higher values, and the other did not. One married a believer, and the other didn't. Before all this happened, Esau had sold his birthright — his family inheritance — to his brother for a meal when he was hungry. As the oldest of the twin brothers, Esau would have inherited most of his father's estate and carried on the family name. However, because he was always after instant gratification and not willing to wait and do what was right, he gave it all away.

We see in this story the anguish his parents felt when Esau married an unbeliever. Any believing parents will experience such anguish because they want the best for their adult children. That's why you have to pray that your adult child will find a husband or wife from the family of believers. Pray also that your adult child will become all he (she) needs to be in the Lord in order to meet a godly and wonderful person to marry. Without the Lord, marriage is the greatest gamble a person can take. There is no way to predict the outcome if you do not invite God to be in charge and ask Him to reveal the right person at the right time.

One of the things we have consistently prayed about in every one of my prayer groups that I have had for parents is that each of our children will grow up to marry a *wonderful, godly, believing* man or woman. To this day, every adult child who has been married so far has been married to a *wonderful, godly, believing* person. When we see who each of these young people have chosen, we praise God, knowing only He could have put the couples together so perfectly.

My husband and I are still praying the same for our own adult children. While we have not seen any weddings yet, I am certain our prayers have resulted in heading off a few mistakes. There were some close calls where they considered marrying someone who turned out to be the wrong person. Not that those were bad people. In fact, they were quite godly, wonderful, believing people. But they were just not the right ones for our adult children. I have faith that God will bring the right person to each of them at the right time. (We just pray it will be within our lifetime.)

Another example in Scripture of a parent's concern and prayer over an adult child's future mate was Abraham. He did not want his son, Isaac, to marry an unbeliever either. This is the same Isaac as in the last example. So we see that Isaac's father, Abraham, had the same concern for him as Isaac later had for his sons, Esau and Jacob.

Abraham wanted to make sure that his son did not marry one of the unbelieving women of the godless Canaanites, but would marry someone from his own faith. So he instructed his most trusted servant to find a wife for Isaac. He said, "I will make you swear by the Lord, the God of heaven and the God of the earth, that you will not take a wife for my son from the daughters of the Canaanites, among whom I dwell; but you shall go to my country and to my family, and take a wife for my son Isaac" (Genesis 24:3–4).

The servant was concerned that the

woman would not be willing to come back with him and thought that Isaac should go with him. But Abraham said no to that for certain reasons, and he told the servant that God had spoken to him and would send His angel on ahead to prepare the way for his servant to find the wife God had for Isaac (Genesis 24:5–7).

Abraham obviously had been communicating with God about this and praying specifically about a wife for his son. He had the leading of the Lord when he instructed his servant to go to the land of his people to find her. So the servant, then, would be following the Lord's leading when going there.

The servant departed as instructed and prayed that God would give him success (Genesis 24:12). When he arrived in the land of Abraham's family and approached the well where the townspeople went to draw water, he asked God to show him who Isaac's wife was to be. He specifically prayed for a sign — that the young woman at the well whom he asked to give him water to drink would not only give *him* water, but also would offer water for his *camels.* If that happened, he would know that this was the woman God had chosen to be Isaac's wife (Genesis 24:13–14).

At the well he met Rebekah — a beautiful

young virgin woman — who had come to draw water. She not only gave the servant water for himself, but she also offered to draw water for his camels (Genesis 24:15–20). And yet even as the woman was drawing water from the well, the servant prayed again silently, waiting to hear from God to make certain this was the woman He had chosen.

Being assured by God that she was the one, the servant gave Rebekah jewelry that had been sent along with him as a gift for her. When he inquired who she was, she explained that she belonged to a family that turned out to be Abraham's family. The servant bowed and worshipped the Lord, thanking Him for leading him directly to this place and to his master's family (Genesis 24:26–27). The servant related the story to Rebekah and her family of how Abraham had promised him that an angel would go with him and give him success in finding Isaac's wife (Genesis 24:28–40).

This beautiful story of a parent praying for the Lord's leading to find the perfect mate for an adult child can be applied to our lives as well. Of course, there were reasons why Isaac couldn't go there to find her himself. And we don't, in our culture, go out and find a wife for our son or a husband for our daughter and arrange a marriage — although that is a tempting thought sometimes. But it's even better that we can seek God about this and ask *Him* to arrange things. We can pray that our adult child will be led to the *right place* at the *right time* in order to meet the *right person.* And we can trust that our prayers will be heard and answered by the Lord.

First of all, we must ask for what we know is God's will. Abraham didn't look for a wife among the unbelievers. He looked for her among the godly — his family. As a believer, our family members are the believers — our brothers and sisters in Christ. Our first prayer should be, "Lord, bring a godly, believing woman into my son's life to be his wife." "Lord, I pray that my daughter will find a godly, believing man to be her husband." If your adult child is already married, pray for his or her spouse to be a godly believer.

Pray That Your Adult Child Will Marry a Person of Purity

The servant of Abraham prayed that Jacob's future wife would be a virgin — a woman of purity. God's will for us is to be sexually pure before marriage. And today there are many people who are. However, in our culture of sexual pollution, loose morals, peer pressure to be promiscuous, and worship of the idols of lust and gratification, there are many more good people who have made mistakes sexually. While the ultimate choice would be a virgin, and that is what you should pray for because it is God's will, do not discount the Lord's power to purify and redeem someone who has made mistakes. That is also God's will — to purify and redeem. God can bring into your son or daughter's life someone who has been purified and redeemed — where past sins have been confessed and repented of and the heart is pure and there is no more moral failure. They have new life, being lived as a person of purity. When God purifies, He does a complete work.

Pray That Your Adult Child Will Marry Someone with Godly Character

Another important thing the servant of Abraham prayed for with regard to Isaac's wife speaks to the nature of Rebekah's character. He wanted to find a woman who would offer to help and provide for a stranger in need. Rebekah was not hesitant to give him water. And she quickly volunteered to give water to his camels without even a second thought. She didn't roll her eyes and move slowly or reluctantly. It was her character to help someone with a kindness. She not only *gave* him what he *asked* for, but *offered* what he had *prayed* for. She gave above and beyond what was polite. With a gracious, kind, and giving nature, Rebekah also offered him lodging for the night (Genesis 24:21–25).

I used to live on a farming ranch when I was young. We raised corn and wheat, but we also raised cattle. We had no electricity and no plumbing. We had gas lanterns and an outhouse. We drew our water out of a well. If we wanted water to drink, we had to take a clean pail out to the well and draw the water up by hand with a rope attached to the pail. If we wanted to take a bath, which was never more than once a week, we had to draw up the water from the well and heat it on the wood burning stove. This was, of course, after we had chopped the wood into small enough pieces to put *in* the wood burning stove. It was extremely hard work. Water is heavy, for any of you who have never pulled it up from a well and carried it to the kitchen to put on your wood burning stove.

Pulling up water from a well is so much work that while you would certainly give a cup of it to a thirsty stranger, you might think twice before offering to bring up buckets of it for his camels. But if you were a compassionate, loving, generous, and extremely thoughtful person like Rebekah, you would do it without hesitation.

Pray that your adult child will marry someone with a gracious, kind, giving, and loving nature.

The Bible says that Rebekah was beautiful. I'm sure that a big part of her beauty was internal, due to her beautiful character. However, there is nothing wrong with asking God for a beautiful wife for your son or a good-looking husband for your daughter. I don't mean they need to be perfect by the world's standards, but that they always be attractive to your son or daughter. Remember that the Lord can take any man or woman and beautify the inner character and spirit of that person. I have seen relatively unattractive people come to the Lord, and when the beautiful Spirit of God dwells in them, they transform into radiantly beautiful and attractive people.

Pray That Your Adult Children Will Have Great In-Laws

Don't forget to pray for your adult children to have good relationships with their in-laws. There are probably no more fragile relationships than those with in-laws, and bad in-law relationships makes for a very uncomfortable, hurtful, and miserable situation. If your adult children are married and have in-laws, pray for those relationships to be good and stable.

Pray also for a great relationship with your daughter-in-law or son-in-law. Ask God to give you special gifts of wisdom, sensitivity, generosity of spirit, and unconditional love in order to be the best mother-in-law or father-in-law possible. Ask Him to show you how much is too much and how little is not enough when it comes to communication, help, and support. Most of all, pray for God's love to flow through you in a way that is clearly evident.

If Your Adult Child Is Already Married

If your adult child is already married to someone wonderful, pray for your daughter-in-law or son-in-law to be blessed in every way. However, if your adult child is married to someone who concerns you, for whatever reason, pray that God will pour out His Spirit upon your son-in-law or daughter-in-law and manifest the fruit of the Spirit in their character, which is love, joy, peace, patience, kindness, goodness, faithfulness, gentleness, and self-control (Galatians 5:22–23). Ask God to give him or her a gracious, generous, beautiful, attractive, and godly character. This is what God wants. And who knows, your prayers may help a young man or woman find the purifying and transformative power of the Lord.

If your adult child is married to someone who seems distant or odd or difficult, or who troubles your adult child and makes him or her very unhappy or afraid, then get out your knee pads, because you have to put in some serious prayer time. Pray everything you have learned to pray for your adult child in this book for your son-in-law or daughter-in-law.

Pray that you will love your son-in-law or daughter-in-law with all your heart. If you feel you don't have that kind of love, ask God to give you *His* love for that person. He will pour His love so fully into your heart that it will flow from you at all times. Pray that he (she) will have a strong committed relationship with the Lord. Whether he (she) has received the Lord yet or not, pray for Christ's character to be formed in him (her). Pray that you will be the best mother-in-law or father-in-law you can possibly be. Pray for your relationship with him (her) to be rich and good. It can be one of the greatest relationships you will ever have, or it can be one of the worst. Don't settle for anything less than great. And don't forget that God can do great things through the power of His love.

Five Ways to Pray for Your Adult Children to Be Good Parents

1. *Pray that they will recognize their children as a gift from God.* "Behold, children are a heritage from the Lord, the fruit of the womb is a reward" (Psalm 127:3).
2. *Pray that they will train up their children in the ways of the Lord.* "Train up a child in the way he should go, and when he is old he will not depart from it" (Proverbs 22:6).
3. *Pray that they will teach their children with love and not anger.* "And you, fathers, do not provoke your children to wrath, but bring them up in the training and admonition of the Lord" (Ephesians 6:4).
4. *Pray that they will be diligent and wise to discipline their children.* "He who spares his rod hates his son, but he who loves him disciplines him promptly" (Proverbs 13:24).
5. *Pray that they will walk in obedience to God's ways in raising their children*

so their prayers will be answered. "And whatever we ask we receive from Him, because we keep His commandments and do those things that are pleasing in His sight" (1 John 3:22).

TEN WAYS TO PRAY FOR YOUR GRANDCHILDREN

1. Pray that they will be healthy and whole in their mind, body, and soul.
2. Pray that they will live free from accident, injury, or disease.
3. Pray that they will always live in peace, security, and love.
4. Pray that they will be protected from anyone with evil intentions to harm them in any way.
5. Pray that they will come to know the Lord early in life in a genuine, deep, and committed way and they will learn to walk in His ways.
6. Pray that they will be disciplined and corrected properly so that they understand consequences for bad behavior.
7. Pray that they will have a humble, repentant, and teachable heart so they will live free of rebellion and

trouble.

8. Pray that you will have wisdom from God as to how to be the best grandparent and faithfully support their parents' wishes.
9. Pray that God will give your grandchildren's parents good health, great stamina, godly wisdom, and amazing patience.
10. Pray that God will show you how to intercede for each grandchild specifically.

You don't need to have grandchildren in order to start praying for them. You can pray all of these ten points of prayer above for them in advance. If you already do have grandchildren, you are blessed and have great purpose in your life. We do not know how many people have become saved, protected, healed, successful, accomplished, and more, all because they had a praying grandmother or grandfather.

I looked in the Bible at some of the prayers of blessing prayed by godly parents over their adult children and came up with a brief summary of them that we parents can pray over our adult children, as well as our grandchildren:

I pray that God will bless you and make you fruitful. I pray that He will multiply you in every way — with children, with success in your work, with increase in your finances, and with a secure home. I pray you will never be a wanderer — not owning or possessing anything of value — but that you will put down roots and possess the land where you dwell. I pray that you will build a good, solid, and secure life always for you and your wife (husband) and your children and grandchildren.

In Jesus' name I pray.

Lord, I pray for (name of adult child) and ask that You would give him (her) the perfect wife (husband). Bring a godly believing woman (man) into his (her) life, who will be with him (her) for the rest of their lives in a fulfilling and happy marriage. I pray that she (he) will have purity of heart, plus a nature and character that is gracious, kind, giving, and loving. I pray that they will always be attracted to one another in a way that is lasting.

For my adult child who is already married, I pray that You will cause him (her) and his (her) mate to increase in love, joy, peace, patience, kindness, goodness, faithfulness, gentleness, and self-control (Galatians 5:22–23). I pray that their hearts will grow together and not apart. Make the necessary changes in them that are needed. Help each one of them to learn to pray in power for one another.

I pray that they will love and honor one another, and learn to submit to one another (1 Peter 5:5). Help them to communicate mutual appreciation and respect. I pray above all that they will "have fervent love for one another, for love will cover a multitude of sins" (1 Peter 4:8). Dwell in their marriage, Lord, and make it what You want it to be.

I pray that forgiveness will flow easily between them and that no negative emotions will spoil the atmosphere of their home. I pray that their hearts will be kind and soft toward one another, and that they will always be each other's top priority. Make their marriage to be a success story so there will be no divorce in their future.

Lord, help my adult child to be the best husband (wife) possible. Teach him (her) the things needed to make a marriage successful. Give him (her) understanding, patience, and the ability to communicate well. I pray that there will be no pride in him (her) that would stir up strife, but rather he (she) would trust in You and be prospered (Proverbs 28:25). Take out of his (her) life anything that would keep him (her) from becoming the husband (wife) You want him (her) to be.

I pray that each of my adult children will themselves have healthy, whole, intelligent, gifted, and godly children. Help them through every step of parenthood and enable them to be successful in raising children who are obedient, bright, healthy, happy, and productive. As parents, give them an abundance of love, patience, understanding, and wisdom. Guide them every step of the way, through every stage of each child's development. I pray that they will look to You for guidance and not the world, so that they will train up their children in Your ways. Teach them how to discipline, correct, guide, and nurture their children properly. Help them to always recognize that their children are a gift from You. I pray that their relationship with each child will be good and lasting.

Protect each of my adult children's children from all harm and any plans of evil. Protect them from injury or disease. I pray that anyone with evil intentions will never be allowed to come near them. Help them to know You and learn to live Your way. Do not allow them to live separated from You. Give them a humble and teachable spirit, and help them to always honor and obey their parents and not fall into rebellion.

Lord, help me to leave a great inheritance to my children and their children in terms of wisdom, godliness, fruitfulness, and wholeness that will bless them for their entire lives (Proverbs 13:22). Help me to live a godly life that pleases You, so that I will not only know Your mercy, but they will know it as well (Psalm 103:17–18).

In Jesus' name I pray.

WORD POWER

What God has joined together, let not man separate.
MATTHEW 19:6

Unless the LORD builds the house, they labor in vain who build it.
PSALM 127:1

The righteous man walks in his integrity; his children are blessed after him.
PROVERBS 20:7

The mercy of the LORD is from everlasting to everlasting on those who fear Him, and His righteousness to children's children, to such as keep His covenant, and to those who remember His commandments to do them.
PSALM 103:17–18

They shall not labor in vain, nor bring forth children for trouble; for they shall be the descendants of the blessed of the LORD, and their offspring with them.
ISAIAH 65:23

12

Pray That Your Adult Children Will Maintain Strong and Fulfilling Relationships

Strong relationships are very important to every one of us. We all need good people around us who strengthen us and contribute to the quality of our lives. And we need our relationships to work out and not become strained and fall apart.

Good relationships are crucial for our adult children. We've all seen what the bad influence of the wrong friends can do — if not in our own children, then we've seen it in others. Even the bad influence of business people with whom they spend a great deal of time at work is cause for much prayer. Unhealthy and unwise relationships can destroy their sense of who God made them to be and lead them off the path God has for them.

There are certain relationships that are vital to their success in life. Besides the relationships with a spouse and in-laws — which I covered in the last chapter — other important relationships are with friends, coworkers, siblings, and parents. They all contribute to a sense of well-being and must be covered in prayer. We can't underestimate the value of having these particular relationships be strong and solid in our adult children's lives.

Pray for Good Relationships with Godly Friends

Our adult children need good, godly friends. It is never healthy for anyone to be too isolated — not emotionally, mentally, spiritually, or physically. People who are too isolated always wind up a little off in their thinking and become a touch weird. This is true whether they are believers or not. But as believers we need people around us who are godly and who have the love of God, the Holy Spirit, and Jesus in them. People like this build us up and help us to keep things in proper perspective.

No matter how strong we think we are, something of the people with whom we spend time rubs off on us — whether good or bad. That's why it is important to make sure our closest relationships are with people who are godly. The Bible says to "not be unequally yoked with unbelievers" (2 Corinthians 6:14). We must pray for our adult children to have godly friends. It's not that they can't ever be around people who are not believers, but the people who are the most influential in their lives should be those who know the Lord.

The Bible says so much about the importance of choosing the right friends that we can't ignore the significance of it. I have seen countless problems in the lives of adult children who spent time with the wrong people. "The righteous should choose his friends carefully, for the way of the wicked leads them astray" (Proverbs 12:26). It can't get any clearer than that. The wrong people will sway us off the path, no matter how much we assure ourselves that this will never happen to us.

If there was one main issue my husband and I had with our adult children, it was that there were times when they allowed the wrong people to become influential in their lives. And those relationships got them off the path God had for them. My adult children were by nature always kind, friendly, and accepting to everyone, and they thought they could handle someone who was a little more worldly, especially when that person was disguised as a Christian. However, they were too young and inexperienced at the time to see through these people and how any relationship with them would lead them to trouble. Through the prayers of parents and prayer group members their eyes were finally opened to see the truth about those particular relationships and they quickly severed them.

Today, even though there are no troublesome friends in their lives, I still pray about this. Bad influences are part of the enemy's plan for our demise, so I keep asking God to give them wisdom, discernment, and revelation about the people they meet and spend time with. The company our adult children keep is one of the most important decisions they will make.

Pray that your adult children will choose their friends carefully so they won't end up being led astray. In this culture where there is so much evil influence, it is hard to know a person's true character unless you have godly wisdom and discernment. Pray for your adult children to have a strong sense of who is a good influence and who isn't. It will help them make the right choices about whom they associate with and trust. The quality of their friendships will affect the quality of their life.

Pray for Good Relationships with Coworkers

I know one young man who was trying to find favor with people *for* whom and *with* whom he worked, who were a worldly, hard-drinking crowd. He tried to keep up, but they were used to that lifestyle and he wasn't. They could hold their liquor and he couldn't. So he came close to becoming an alcoholic. Associating with them ended up costing him nearly everything, including his good reputation, not to mention the trust of the people who were most important to him. He also sacrificed a few years of his life and experienced a setback in his career.

He had praying parents who came to his rescue once it was revealed to them what was happening. They could see by the way he looked that something was wrong, but they had no hard evidence. They first called on a few close and trusted believing friends to support them in prayer. Then they and their pastor confronted him, just at the time when his life was beginning to fall apart. It was a horribly painful thing for everyone concerned, but through this time of loving confrontation and ongoing prayer, this young man's life was turned around.

I give this example because no one would

have thought that such a thing could ever happen to this particular young man. He was a godly believer who had been raised in a good, believing home. This all happened because of the company he kept due to his work relationships. These were not friends he chose, but coworkers he was trying to impress and with whom he felt he needed to find acceptance.

Pray that your adult children find favor with the people *for* whom and *with* whom they work without having to compromise anything of what is right in the sight of God. Of course, if they can't get along with others they will have problems sustaining a good, lasting, and successful career, but getting along doesn't mean throwing out what they know are God's ways. Pray for them to have the respect of their coworkers *because* of their godly lifestyle.

Pray for Good Relationships with Brothers and Sisters

It is important for everyone to have good relationships with their brothers and sisters. (If your adult child is an only child, there is probably a cousin or other family member who is like a brother or sister to him or her.) I have always prayed for my children to have a good relationship with one another, and I am grateful to see that they are very close to this day. I am certain that after I and my husband are gone, they will continue to be close. I have seen too many siblings grow up and seldom see each other again. And once the parents are gone, they never have any communication. Many people don't realize how important family ties are to their well-being.

It may go without saying, but it is so important to not exhibit favoritism with your children. It only breeds resentment and hatred, and it fractures family unity. Many people aren't aware when they are playing favorites, but the adult children certainly are. Sometimes one child may be much easier to be with or get along with than another. If you have a favorite, ask God to give you equal love for your adult children just as He has for His. Ask Him to help you to demonstrate equal love for each of them in a way that they can clearly see.

A perfect example of a parent having a favorite among his children was Isaac, who was later called Israel. "Israel loved Joseph more than all his children, because he was the son of his old age. Also he made him a tunic of many colors. But when his brothers saw that their father loved him more than all his brothers, they hated him and could not speak peaceably to him" (Genesis 37:3–4).

Jacob's favoring his young son Joseph caused great resentment among his brothers. Added to that, Joseph told his brothers about a dream he had that suggested his brothers would one day bow down to him. Then "his brothers envied him" and they "conspired against him to kill him" (Genesis 37:11,18). But slave traders came along, and Joseph's brothers sold Joseph to them instead of killing him (Genesis 37:28). This was a horrible situation that God later turned into something good because of the godliness of Joseph. In the end, he and his brothers were reconciled, the family was reunited, and Joseph saved them all from a severe famine in the land.

If you have a blended family with children from a different mother or father as Joseph did — he and his brothers had the same father, but four different mothers — or stepchildren blended with your children, pray that there not be jealousy among them. Ask God to help you avoid showing any favoritism that would cause resentment. Favoritism will always result in a death of some kind — the death of a relationship, the death of love and kindness, and the death of family — because after you and the other parent of those children die, the family will completely fall apart. I have seen these results in families far too often, and it is very sad. Pray that this does not happen to your family. Pray for good relationships between all of your children so that after you are gone they won't be left feeling adrift. Everyone needs this sense of family more than they fully realize.

Pray that your children don't end up jealous of one another for *any* reason. Make out your will and be sure that everything is equally divided — even if you have little in the way of riches. I have seen siblings fighting over the smallest inheritance that was either not clearly stated in a will, or it was clearly written out in a legal document that revealed hurtful favoritism. These brothers and sisters were divided and devastated for the rest of their lives.

Conflict and competitiveness between siblings is damaging and can be enslaving to everyone involved — enslavement to resentment, bitterness, anger, hatred, feelings of rejection, and distrust — which results in fractured family relationships. If that has already happened in some way in your family, pray to break that spirit of division. Ask God to heal the fractures and restore those sibling relationships.

"Therefore if you bring your gift to the altar, and there remember that your brother has something against you, leave your gift there before the altar, and go your way. First be reconciled to your brother, and then come and offer your gift" (Matthew 5:23–24).

If nothing like that has happened in your family, ask God to help you make sure it never does. Anything that destroys relationships between your adult children will help to fulfill the enemy's plan for their destruction.

Pray for Good Relationships with Parents

One of the greatest blessings your adult children will ever receive is to have a godly friend in you. You will always be their mom or dad, but when they establish their own lives and are not dependant upon you, you have to ask God to help you find the perfect balance of being loving, but not smothering; encouraging, but not indulging; concerned, but not critical; caring, but not controlling; building up, but not overbearing; supportive, but not disabling. Only God can help you walk that sensitive line.

If your relationship with your adult child has been damaged — or it has been damaged with his or her other parent — know that God can restore it and that He desires to do so. All relationships are vulnerable to destruction without God holding them together against enemy attacks. The enemy wants to destroy our relationships because he knows that weakens us and does not please God.

The enemy's desire is to bring confusion to relationships and cause misinterpretation of words, actions, or intentions. He blinds people to the truth and feeds them lies. He knows how to separate people from God and from each other. But God's power is far greater than the enemy's. The enemy only wins in our lives when he can get us to believe a lie about God.

Every time you pray for your adult children, remember that they always have an enemy who wants to see them blinded, deceived, brought down, and destroyed. The Bible is crystal clear about the existence of Satan and his intentions in our lives. But the Bible also says that Jesus conquered death and hell on the cross. That means He defeated the enemy's ability to control our lives. *When you are praying about something that seems hopeless or absolutely unchanging in your adult children's lives, remember that you are not at war with them; you are at war with the enemy who is the god of this age who blinds people to the truth* (2 Corinthians 4:3–4).

The Lord can bring to life any relationship that has died. He can mend a relationship that has been broken. He can reconnect a relationship that has been severed. Your prayers can turn things around and help that happen. Your prayers can promote forgiveness, restoration, and healing where it is needed.

Even in the family line of King David — through whom the Messiah would later come — there were fractured and strained relationships. Yet God brought great good out of that family line in the birth of His Son, Jesus. God will do the same in your relationship with your adult children and their relationships with other family members as well. He will respond to your prayers for reconciliation. Nothing is beyond the reach of God's grace, the promises of God's Word, or the reach of the Savior's hand extended toward you and your adult children. God can break through our stubbornness, pride, hurt, unforgiveness, anger, and pain. He can put any relationship your adult children have with either parent back together again and birth something new and great in the process.

Show the love of God to your adult children with the words you speak to them. "Let your speech always be with grace, seasoned with salt, that you may know how you ought to answer each one" (Colossians 4:6). Ask God to give you wisdom whenever you speak to them so that your words are not critical and wounding in any way. "There is one who speaks like the piercings of a sword, but the tongue of the wise promotes health" (Proverbs 12:18). Ask God to show you how to shine His light of unconditional love for each of them (Matthew 5:14–16).

If you are praying from afar, tell them how you are praying as an encouragement. Make it a positive affirmation. Don't say, "I'm praying for you and that wife of yours to stop making stupid decisions about your finances." Say instead, "I'm praying for God to pour out abundance upon you two in every way." Don't say, "I'm praying for you to wake up and get rid of your hoodlum friends." Say instead, "I am praying for you to have wisdom and revelation from God so that you will always make the right decisions."

Adult children always benefit from any blessings you speak on their lives, so speak blessings over them whenever you are with them. Say something like, "I'm praying that

God will open doors for you that no man can close." Or, "I'm praying that God will use the gifts and talents He has put in you for His glory."

Just because they are older now doesn't mean your adult children don't need your love and emotional support anymore. They may act as though they don't because they want you to know they can handle their lives themselves, but the truth is they need it far more than they may say. The issues they face are bigger and the opposition is fiercer. Pray for all their relationships to be strong, but especially with you and their other parent or stepparents.

Pray that your adult children will never be brought down by unforgiveness and bitterness in any of their relationships, but rather that forgiveness will flow like water from a well in their hearts.

PRAYER POWER

Lord, I pray for (name of adult child) to have godly friends in her (his) life. I pray that they will be a positive influence on her (him). Enable her (him) to see the truth about people and be drawn toward those who are good. Give her (him) the strength and wisdom to separate herself (himself) from anyone who is not a good influence. Take out of her (his) life anyone who is a bad influence and who draws her (him) away from You and Your ways (1 Corinthians 5:11).

I pray she (he) will have friends who tell her (him) the truth in love (Proverbs 27:6) and will give her (him) good advice and guidance (Proverbs 27:9). I pray for friends who are wise (Proverbs 13:20) and will always be a strong support for her (him) (Ecclesiastes 4:9–10). I pray that each relationship in her (his) life will be glorifying to You, Lord.

Along with friends, I pray especially for good relationships with parents, siblings, and other family members. Bless these relationships with deep love, great compassion, mutual understanding, and good communication. Where there are breeches or rough spots in any one of those relationships, I pray that You would bring peace, healing, and reconciliation. I pray that the enemy will not be able to break apart any family relationships or friendships.

I pray specifically for her (his) relationship with (name of person). I pray that You would heal any breach or strain between them and bring harmony by the power of Your Holy Spirit. Where there has been miscommunication, bring clarity and good communication. Where there has been a rightful grievance, bring repentance and apologies. Wherever the relationship has broken down, for whatever reason, bring healing and restoration.

I pray that she (he) will always have good relationships with coworkers. Where there is a coworker who is ungodly, I pray that my adult child will be a godly influence on that person. Help her (him) to stand strong and not be weak with intimidation. I pray that she (he) will walk with the wise and become wiser, and not be a "companion of fools" and be destroyed (Proverbs 13:20).

Help her (him) to learn the obedience of forgiveness. Enable her (him) to forgive easily and not carry grudges, resentment, bitterness, or a personal list of wrongs. Help her (him) to release unforgiveness quickly to others, so that it never interferes with her (his) relationship with You and delay the forgiveness she (he) must have to enrich her (his) own life (Mark 11:25).

In Jesus' name I pray.

He who walks with wise men will be wise, but the companion of fools will be destroyed.
PROVERBS 13:20

I am a companion of all who fear You, and of those who keep Your precepts.
PSALM 119:63

Do not be unequally yoked together with unbelievers. For what fellowship has righteousness with lawlessness? And what communion has light with darkness? And what accord has Christ with Belial? Or what part has a believer with an unbeliever?
2 CORINTHIANS 6:14–15

Do not enter the path of the wicked, and do not walk in the way of evil.
PROVERBS 4:14

But if we walk in the light as He is in the light, we have fellowship with one another, and the blood of Jesus Christ His Son cleanses us from all sin.
1 JOHN 1:7

13
Pray That Your Adult Children Will Be Protected and Survive Tough Times

Before they are even born, one of the first prayers we pray for our children is for their protection. And we continue to pray about that nearly every day from then on. The most important concern of any parent is that their child be protected from serious injury and disease. We also want them protected from evil people who desire to do criminal acts against them. And we definitely want them protected from early death. We pray for them to outlive us and enjoy a long and healthy life. It doesn't matter how old your child is — you can be 99 and your adult child 81 — protection will always be a concern. That's why praying for God's protection over them is the only way to ever have peace about that.

My sister, Suzy, and I have been in a weekly prayer group together with some other women for nearly 20 years. Every week we pray specifically for each one of our now adult children. Suzy's daughter — my niece, Stephanie — is the same age as my daughter, Amanda. They are actually only two weeks apart. One of the greatest blessings has been seeing them grow up together. The one thing we have always prayed about for them was that God would protect them.

When Stephanie was in her early twenties and married less than a year, her husband, Jeremy, who had graduated from West Point and was an officer in the army, was deployed to Iraq for a year of duty. (May I add that Jeremy is definitely a wonderful answer to our prayers for a godly and perfect husband for Stephanie.) When the troops left the community where they lived near the army base, it became like a ghost town, with nearly all of the men gone and many of the women and children moved back home with their parents. Stephanie was living alone in their house and feeling very vulnerable because of that. She had been a part of my prayer group for a few years, so she asked us to especially cover her in prayer for safety during this time.

At each of our prayer group meetings, we usually read the Word, have a time of worship, and then we cover ourselves and all of our immediate family members by name in a prayer for safety and protection. But this particular week we made special mention of both Jeremy fighting in a dangerous war zone and Stephanie home alone in a town with few people left in it.

The thing you need to know about Stephanie is that she is probably the most conscientious, organized, and responsible person I know. But one afternoon she went shopping for groceries and came home to hear the phone ringing and the dogs barking. She was especially diligent to never miss a call in case it was her husband calling from Iraq, so she ran in the door, quickly put her groceries on the counter, and hurried to answer her phone. After she finished the call, she put her groceries away and made dinner for herself. Once she had eaten, fed the dogs, and cleaned up the kitchen, it was time to get ready for bed. She made sure all the doors were locked and all the lights were off, except for the front porch light, and then she went into her bedroom and got into bed.

But she couldn't fall asleep right away.

She kept feeling more and more uneasy about her safety. She felt strongly led to pray specifically that God would protect her and the other women staying alone in their houses on her street that night. She also prayed fervently for her husband's safety. She wondered if it was for him that she felt led to pray so intensely, but the more she prayed, the more she felt it was for her own safety that she needed to be praying.

When she woke up the next morning, she went to her front door as she usually did to retrieve the newspaper on the front steps. The moment she opened the door she was horrified to see her house keys, with the car keys attached, still in the lock of the front door. They had been sitting in the front door lock — only a few feet from the street and with the front porch light illuminating them — all night long. Anyone could have just walked in the house and there would have been no one to stop him. Stephanie knew that God had led her to pray that night for her own safety, and she knew it was God who had protected her. She immediately called the prayer group members and told us what had happened. We all knew God had answered our many prayers for her safety.

Ten Ways to Pray About Protection for Your Adult Children

1. *Pray that your adult children have the*

wisdom and good judgment to do the right thing. Their wisdom will keep them out of harm's way more than we will ever know. "The LORD gives wisdom; from His mouth come knowledge and understanding; He stores up sound wisdom for the upright; He is a shield to those who walk uprightly; He guards the paths of justice, and preserves the way of His saints" (Proverbs 2:6–8).

2. *Pray that your adult children will learn to fear God and not man.* When they have a fear of man it causes them to do stupid, ungodly, and regrettable things. "The fear of man brings a snare, but whoever trusts in the LORD shall be safe" (Proverbs 29:25).
3. *Pray that your adult children will trust God and His Word.* Trusting in the ways of God will keep them on the right path. "Every word of God is pure; He is a shield to those who put their trust in Him" (Proverbs 30:5).
4. *Pray that your adult children will live in the presence of God where there is safety.* When they invite God to dwell in the secret places of their

heart, they will live in His protective shadow, hidden away from danger. "He who dwells in the secret place of the Most High shall abide under the shadow of the Almighty" (Psalm 91:1).

5. *Pray that your adult children will make God their refuge and turn to Him for protection.* Then they can trust God to deliver them from danger and all attacks of the enemy. "I will say of the LORD, 'He is my refuge and my fortress; my God, in Him I will trust.' Surely He shall deliver you from the snare of the fowler and from the perilous pestilence" (Psalm 91:2–3).
6. *Pray that your adult children will be hidden in the Lord and use His Word as their shield.* They must recognize that God's Word acts as a protective barrier shielding them from enemy onslaught. "He shall cover you with His feathers, and under His wings you shall take refuge; His truth shall be your shield and buckler" (Psalm 91:4).
7. *Pray that your adult children will not live in fear of danger or disease.* When they keep their eye on God,

they will not have to live in fear of the attacks that can occur anytime, day or night. "You shall not be afraid of the terror by night, nor of the arrow that flies by day, nor of the pestilence that walks in darkness, nor of the destruction that lays waste at noonday" (Psalm 91:5–6).

8. *Pray that your adult children will not be afraid, even when they see destruction happening around them.* This is not living in denial; it's knowing that because they are walking with God, He has their back. "A thousand may fall at your side, and ten thousand at your right hand; but it shall not come near you" (Psalm 91:7).
9. *Pray that your adult children will understand the consequences for not living God's way.* So many people don't understand that there is a price to pay for disobedience, and it will one day come upon them. The reward for disobedience is no reward at all. "Only with your eyes shall you look, and see the reward of the wicked" (Psalm 91:8).
10. *Pray that your adult children will understand that the reward for living*

God's way is His protection. When they live God's way, He will keep them on the right path, out of harm's way, protected from evil, injury, and disease. "Because you have made the LORD, who is my refuge, even the Most High, your dwelling place, no evil shall befall you, nor shall any plague come near your dwelling" (Psalm 91:9–10).

Pray That God Will Surround Your Adult Child with Angels

The Bible has a lot to say about angels. And specifically the ones that protect us. Here are a few great examples of the appearing of angels:

The angel of the Lord appeared a number of times to Joseph, the husband of Mary, concerning where they should go to be safe. The angel instructed Mary and Joseph to leave Bethlehem with Jesus. "An angel of the Lord appeared to Joseph in a dream, saying, 'Arise, take the young Child and His mother, flee to Egypt, and stay there until I bring you word; for Herod will seek the young Child to destroy Him' " (Matthew 2:13).

An angel of the Lord entered Peter's cell and rescued him. In an earlier chapter in this book I described how an angel delivered Peter to freedom in a way that was humanly impossible. "Now behold, *an angel of the Lord* stood by him, and a light shone in the prison; and he struck Peter on the side and raised him up, saying, 'Arise quickly!' And his chains fell off his hands . . . and they went out and went down one street, and immediately the angel departed from him. And when Peter had come to himself, he said, 'Now I know for certain *that the Lord has sent His angel, and has delivered me* from the hand of Herod and from all the expectation of the Jewish people' " (Acts 12:7–11, emphasis added).

An angel came to the apostle Paul in the middle of a hurricane. The angel spoke to Paul about what would and would not happen to him. Paul was kept safe and what was predicted happened just as the angel said. "For there stood by me this night an angel of the God to whom I belong and whom I serve, saying, 'Do not be afraid, Paul; you must be brought before Caesar; and indeed God has granted you all those who sail with you' " (Acts 27:23–24).

Jesus told of how important the guardian angels of our children are.

The disciples were asking Jesus who was the greatest in the kingdom of heaven

(Matthew 18:1). Then Jesus called a child to him and told them, "Whoever humbles himself as this little child is the greatest in the kingdom of heaven. Whoever receives one little child like this in My name receives Me" (Matthew 18:4–5). Jesus went on to say, "Take heed that you do not despise one of these little ones, for I say to you that *in heaven their angels always see the face of My Father who is in heaven*" (Matthew 18:10, emphasis added). God assigns guardian angels to care for our children.

There is no place in the Bible that says these guardian angels say to the child once he or she is ten or twelve, "Okay, my job is done. You're on your own now. Good luck and try not to do anything stupid." No, Jesus says of children that it is not the will of their Father in heaven that any one of them should perish (Matthew 18:1–14). That speaks to me that the harm, destruction, death, or loss of any child in any way is the work of the enemy and not the will of God.

Your adult child is still just as important to God as when he or she was a young child. But as an adult, they are at the age where they make their own decisions as to whether they will live God's way or not, or whether they will be repentant or rebellious.

In the Bible, angels are referred to as "*ministering spirits* sent forth to minister for those who will inherit salvation" (Hebrews 1:14, emphasis added). It also says, "For *He shall give His angels charge over you, to keep you in all your ways.* In their hands they shall bear you up, lest you dash your foot against a stone" (Psalm 91:11–12, emphasis added). When we read those two verses above in light of the rest of Psalm 91, we can see that God will give His angels charge over us to protect us *when we live His way.* If we want the protection of angels, we must live within the boundaries and under the umbrella of God's protection. We must dwell with the Lord and make Him our refuge. This is exactly what we must pray for with regard to our adult children.

Pray for Your Adult Children to Have a Long and Fruitful Life

We never want to outlive our children. And we don't want to die young. We want to live to see our young children become adult children and live long, healthy, and fruitful lives. We want to see our children's children grow up. God gives our adult children a way to have a long and blessed life, and that is to love and obey Him. "Because he has set his love upon Me, therefore I will deliver him; I will set him on high, because he has known My name. He shall call upon Me, and I will answer him; I will be with him in trouble; I will deliver him and honor him. With long life I will satisfy him, and show him My salvation" (Psalm 91:14–16).

The fifth of the Ten Commandments is the first commandment with a promise. It says, "Honor your father and your mother, that *your days may be long* upon the land which the LORD your God is giving you" (Exodus 20:12, emphasis added). Honoring you as their parent is another way for your adult children to obey God and have a long and fruitful life.

When the apostle Paul instructed all children to obey their parents, he said they should honor them *"that it may be well with you* and *you may live long on the earth"* (Ephesians 6:1–3, emphasis added). A child who honors both his (her) father and mother will see his (her) life go well and last long. Again, I don't see a cutoff point where God says, "You're a grown-up now, so you don't have to honor your parents anymore." This promise is for all of our lives. If an adult child dishonors his (her) parents at any age, he (she) will not see the long, successful, and fulfilling life God has for him (her).

Children must be *taught* to honor their parents, not only out of love and respect for them, but also out of the fear of the Lord. They need to recognize clearly what God expects of them and have a desire to please Him. If your adult child treats you with disrespect, or regards you as someone to be tolerated as opposed to cherished, pray immediately for a change of heart in him or her. If your child got away with being disrespectful to you when they were young, it is likely they are still that way now. However, it doesn't matter how old he (she) is. You shouldn't allow it.

It's always powerful when one parent stands up for the other. I love it when I see a dad say, "Don't talk to your mother that way." This can be done with adult children as well as small children. If you allow your adult child to dishonor you or the other parent, you are contributing to their downfall. It's not about getting a good Mother's Day or Father's Day gift; it's about them showing you respect, appreciation, and honor.

I have a friend who is a believer but her husband is not. I will call her Abby and her husband John. John's first wife left him and their two very young children, whom he then raised all by himself. Years later when Abby met John, the children were about eight and ten years old. After Abby and John were married, she raised the children as her own. Now they are grown and in their late thirties.

Although these adult children have always honored Abby as their mother, especially on Mother's Day, they had a falling out with their father. John gave them his opinion about some aspect of their lives, but it was not welcome and so they stopped speaking to him. Both last year and this, they did not even call or send a card to him on Father's Day, his birthday, or Christmas. Of course, he has been terribly hurt by it.

John is almost 70, and only God knows how much time any of us have left on this earth. It is heartbreaking for Abby to see how her adult children have dishonored their father, who dedicated his entire life to them and gave up so much to raise them. Not only have they done great harm to him, but they are also shutting off blessings in their own lives.

If I were in Abby's situation, I would call each of the children and explain the harm that is being done. But first I would pray this way:

> Lord, it grieves me to see how my husband has been dishonored by his own

children. I pray that You would help his heart to heal from the hurt and be able to completely forgive them. Turn the hearts of these adult children toward their father. I pray that they will be led to apologize to him, and he to them for anything they have done to offend one another. I pray that complete reconciliation will happen between them. Show me what I can do or say to either of our adult children or their father to help this situation. Convict their hearts about this before the full consequences of dishonoring their father come to fruition. I pray for complete restoration of these relationships.

If we want our adult children to have a long and fruitful life, we have to pray for and encourage them to honor us as parents. We don't want their lives to be shortened or minimized in any way. We must pray also for ourselves that we will be easy for them to love and honor, and not difficult. Love is the greatest avenue by which to inspire honor. Say to the Lord, "Teach me how I can show love for my adult children in a way that inspires honor."

Sometimes there are situations so bad that honoring a parent is a difficult thing. But it still must be done. I know a Christian woman who is now a single mom because her husband had horrendous problems with pornography and she couldn't allow her children to be exposed to that influence. While a number of men have been delivered from that and able to find healing, he was not one of them. She continued to teach her children to honor him as their father, even though they did not know the truth about why their parents divorced. When her son was almost a teenager, he confessed to his mother that his dad had been showing him pornography and sexually abusing him. She was devastated and has had all parental rights taken away from her ex-husband. She was a godly woman, trying to do the right thing by teaching her children to honor their father, and the father completely dishonored himself. Sometimes a parent has to be honored from afar.

The fact that you need to require your adult children to honor you as their parent doesn't mean you are saying, "Give me honor or else." It's that you need to draw the boundaries when necessary and show your adult children where respect ends and disrespect begins. We must also ask God to help us be so deserving of respect that we never have to demand it.

As we have raised our children, my husband and I have seen how planting one small seed can grow into something big — either for good or for bad, for building up or tearing down, to send a child in one direction or another. We can plant seeds in our children. When we say things to our adult children that build them up, help them to see their good qualities and their great potential and purpose, and give them a sense of their own worth, then we won't have to worry about them honoring us. They will just do it out of love and gratitude. Let's ask God to help us plant good seeds.

Pray That Your Adult Children Will Survive Tough Times

We parents are very concerned when we see our adult children go through difficult times. We suffer with them, and we don't want them to hurt. But God uses the tough times we all go through for good when we walk with Him through them. That means we will not always be protected *from* hard times, but *in* them. We need to pray every day that our adult children recognize that "the name of the LORD is a strong tower; the righteous run to it and are safe" (Proverbs 18:10). Pray that they will always run to the name of Jesus, where they will find protection, strength, and safety.

Many times God will allow us to go through tough times to get our attention or to adjust our way. God permits suffering in our lives as a way of disciplining us and preparing us for what is ahead. "Whom the LORD loves He chastens, and scourges every son whom He receives" (Hebrews 12:6). The ultimate purpose of the suffering God allows in our lives is to restore us to right relationship to Him.

None of us can stand to see our children suffer, however, and when we do, we want to rush in and fix everything. But we can't play God. We have to ask the Lord to show us what is actually happening. If you have been praying that God will get your adult child's attention and do what it takes to get him or her on the right path, and then some kind of misery happens, it could be an answer to your prayers.

Of course, we don't want our adult children to suffer needlessly, or be injured, ruined, or destroyed. We must help them when help is needed, but we have to ask God for wisdom and discernment about that. Sometimes an adult child has to learn a hard lesson. Ask God to give you direction and insight. And no matter what is going on, ask God to help your adult child glean whatever he or she needs to learn from the experience.

When we are in the middle of a difficult situation, we always look forward to the day when it will be over and we can get on with our lives. But God wants us to know that our lives *are* getting on right then. He wants us to know that He is with us all through those tough times when we ask Him to be, and that means there are good things happening whether we can see them at the moment or not. God wants us to trust Him to lead us through it and out of it. We must pray for our adult child to understand all this. We probably need to pray for ourselves to better understand it as well, because sometimes it is hard to remember these things when we are in the middle of a trial.

If something bad has happened to one of your adult children, know that there is no situation so severe that the power of God can't move in it to bring him or her back from trouble to a life of restoration and blessing. When you pray for your adult children through a difficult time, they can come out on the other side in better shape than before and with a far deeper relationship with God.

Sometimes there is no easy way out of a problem, and you and your adult child have to deal with it head-on. Because, let's face it, *we* go through these things with our adult children even when we try to pretend it's all *their* problem. Just remember that when God is brought into the situation in prayer, all things will work together for good. If the suffering your adult child is experiencing is the work of the enemy, pray that God will redeem the situation and restore what has been damaged. Total restoration is what living the life God has for us through Jesus Christ is all about. His will is to restore our entire being and our entire life. He wants that degree of restoration for our adult children as well.

Pray That Your Adult Children Understand the Goodness of God

One of the many things I learned from my longtime pastor, Jack Hayford, was to tell our children stories about ourselves, our family, or them, that can enrich their understanding of the goodness of the Lord and His ways. "I will open my mouth in a parable; I will utter dark sayings of old, which we have heard and known, and our fathers have told us. We will not hide them from their children, telling to the generation to come the praises of the LORD, and His strength and His wonderful works that He has done" (Psalm 78:2–4).

One of the stories I like to tell my children — and now my adult children — is how my dad had a praying mother. She was a devoted Christian who prayed for her eight children, and we have personally seen the fruit of those prayers for my dad.

My father escaped death so many times in his life that the stories are almost unbelievable. I have often heard these stories from him, from other family members, and from old family friends, and he told them repeatedly to my children. One time I interviewed him for nearly two hours about these events and recorded our conversation on tape so that I would always have a record of it. Here are ten ways in which my father escaped death during his lifetime:

1. He was struck by lightning when he was 14.
2. He had such a serious case of pleurisy when he was young that a doctor had to stick a knife through his side and into his lung to drain it — all without any anesthetic.
3. He was shot in the head accidentally by a man with a rifle.
4. He fell into a deep ravine in the middle of a blizzard when he was

on horseback — horse and all. He would have frozen to death if someone hadn't come looking for him and was able to find him and pull him out. (The horse, sadly, didn't make it.)

5. He drove off a cliff in his truck while traveling down a winding, snowed-over mountain road that had become icy. He fell headlong about 50 feet and ended up in a snowbank that broke his fall. He was able to drive through the snowbank and across a prairie until he found a road.
6. He had a serious heart attack.
7. He was hit by a train that demolished his car.
8. He was struck by lightning a second time — although not in the same place.
9. He was attacked by an angry bull.
10. He almost drowned in a river when the horse he was riding fell on top of him and his leg was trapped underneath it.

I can't prove that having a praying mother is why my father survived all of these near-death experiences, but no one can prove that this is *not* the reason either. I saw the hole in his side from the pleurisy. And I saw the scar where the bullet struck his head. I saw him in the hospital shortly after he had his heart attack. I also saw the car he was driving after it was hit by a train. I was ten years old at the time, and even at that young age and not knowing the Lord, I thought it was a miracle. The car was so destroyed that I couldn't see how he wasn't killed. The train struck the car on the passenger side and the entire right side of his car was crumpled into the driver's side. I remember looking at that car and wondering how my dad, who was a large man, could possibly have fit in the small space that was left for him. And he didn't have a scratch on him. In fact, in all these incidents, he didn't have any lasting physical damage — except a couple scars — and not a single broken bone.

Any one of these dangers could have killed him, but he died in his sleep in his own bed when he was 93, still with a sound mind and no known disease or sickness. It was the way he always wanted to die.

How does all this happen? My dad wasn't a man to take chances. He just lived a hard-working life the best he knew how, often in difficult circumstances. Oh, and I forgot to say that he survived my mentally ill abusive mother — who would have killed a lesser man long ago. How could he possibly survive all these near-death experiences? I believe it was because he had a praying mother. She died in old age, and all of her eight children went on to live well into old age as well.

My dad is my greatest example of how the prayers of a praying parent can protect a child, and later an adult child, for all of their life and get them through tough times. Your prayers for your adult child can do the same.

Lord, I pray for Your hand of protection to be over my adult children. I pray that they will put their trust in You as their Shield and Protector (Proverbs 30:5). Protect them physically from all accidents, diseases, infirmity, acts of violence by others, sudden dangers, and the plans of evil. Be their protector when ever they are in a car, plane, bus, boat, or any other means of transportation. Wherever they walk, I pray that their feet do not slip; lead them far away from danger (Psalm 17:5). Keep them safe at all times.

I pray that You would surround them with Your angels to keep watch over them so that they will not stumble (Psalm 91:12). Help them to hear Your voice leading them, and teach them to obey You so that they will always be in Your will and at the right place at the right time. I pray that "the fear of the LORD" will be for them a "fountain of life" that will serve to turn them "away from the snares of death" (Proverbs 14:27).

I pray that You will keep Your eyes on them and that they will not take their eyes off of You. Help them to learn to dwell in Your shadow and under Your umbrella of protection (Psalm 91:1). I pray that You will be their "refuge and strength" and their "very present help in trouble" (Psalm 46:1). I pray that no weapon formed against them will prosper (Isaiah 54:17). Be merciful to them and give them safety "in the shadow of Your wings" until such time as all "these calamities have passed by" (Psalm 57:1). Give them the wisdom, discernment, and revelation they need in order to stay safe and not fall into danger.

Lord, You have said in Your Word that even though evil people try to destroy the righteous, You will not allow it (Psalm 37:32–33). Protect my adult children from any plans of evil. Protect them from legal problems, for justice comes from You (Proverbs 29:26). Be with them when they pass through deep waters and keep the river from overflowing them. Enable them to not be burned or consumed in the fire (Isaiah 43:2).

Lord, I pray when they go through tough times, You will be their defender. I pray that they will learn to look to You to be their help (Psalm 121:1–2). The enemy's strength is nothing in light of Your great power. Arm them with strength for the battle and keep them safe (Psalm 18:39). Help them to "cast off the works of darkness, and . . . put on the armor of light" (Romans 13:12). I pray that they will learn to cry out to You in their trouble, so You will deliver them out of their distresses (Psalm 107:6).

I pray that the difficult things they go through will be used for Your glory and for the deepening of their relationship with You. Help them not to lose heart but to believe that they will see Your goodness in their lives and in every situation (Psalm 27:13). No matter what happens, I pray they will ultimately be able to say, "This was the LORD'S doing; it is marvelous in our eyes" (Psalm 118:23). Help them to understand that they can "lie down in peace, and sleep; for You alone, O LORD," make them to "dwell in safety" (Psalm 4:8).

In Jesus' name I pray.

When you pass through the waters, I will be with you; and through the rivers, they shall not overflow you. When you walk through the fire, you shall not be burned, nor shall the flame scorch you.
ISAIAH 43:2

The LORD shall preserve your going out and your coming in from this time forth, and even forevermore.
PSALM 121:8

Yea, though I walk through the valley of the shadow of death, I will fear no evil; for You are with me; Your rod and Your staff, they comfort me.
PSALM 23:4

This poor man cried out, and the LORD heard him, and saved him out of all his troubles.
PSALM 34:6

The LORD is my rock and my fortress and my deliverer; my God, my strength, in whom I will trust; my shield and the horn of my salvation, my stronghold. I will call upon the LORD, who is worthy to be praised; so shall I be saved from

my enemies.
PSALM 18:2–3

14

Pray That Your Adult Children Will Walk into the Future God Has for Them

There is no magic moment when you are no longer involved with your adult children and you can watch the story of their lives unfold like an uplifting movie. You only *think* you can stop being concerned about their future once they are out of school or once they have a secure job or once they can afford to buy a house or once they get past major disappointments or once they meet a nice person to marry or once they *are* married or once they are successful or once they have children of their own or once they get well or once they get right with the Lord or once they get rid of those bad friends or once they get free of that destructive habit or once they figure life out or once they stop pursuing the wrong dream or once they figure out who God made them to be.

Someone asked me recently if having adult children was a life sentence. I said it only felt like I was doing hard time when I wasn't praying. When I'm praying, I see it more like a lifetime assignment from God to keep my adult children covered, so that His will can be done in their lives. But there are some things we should always remember that will encourage us to keep praying, and help us to find peace while waiting for God to answer.

Remember God's Promise for Your Adult Child's Future

What God's Word says about your adult child's future is what He says about your future too. "I know the thoughts that I think toward you, says the LORD, *thoughts of peace and not of evil, to give you a future and a hope.* Then *you will call upon Me and go and pray to Me,* and *I will listen to you.* And *you will seek Me and find Me,* when you *search for Me with all your heart*" (Jeremiah 29:11–13, emphasis added).

Notice the connection between the promise of a peaceful, hope-filled future and prayer. Again it is prayer that appropriates the promise. God is saying that if you seek Him and search for Him with all your heart, you will find Him and the great future He has for you.

As parents of adult children, we can't allow ourselves to dwell on the negatives. We have to control our thoughts and fears and not let worry get the best of us. If we don't, our concerned thoughts about our adult child's future can rob us of joy and make us sick in our bodies, minds, and souls. It will become a bondage from which *we,* then, will need to be delivered. We don't have to live that way when we can pray.

One of the purest forms of prayer is praise. We can drown out all fear about the future with worship. When we worship God, we are touching Him and His kingdom, and in response the Spirit of God touches *us.* Praise and worship is the surest way to invite the presence of God into our lives and our hearts. In His presence we can find liberty from all fear about the future.

Remember That You Always Have Hope in the Lord

Hope keeps us going. It is what gets us up in the morning. It's what keeps us praying. Hope is not wishing on a star for something; it's believing in the promises of God. "Hope does not disappoint, because the love of God has been poured out in our hearts by the Holy Spirit who was given to us" (Romans 5:5). God's love in us inspires hope, which inspires prayer and the faith to believe.

The enemy tries to steal our hope about the future with his lies, but we can silence him with the Word of God and find joy in the process. "You have made known to me the ways of life; You will make me full of joy in Your presence" (Acts 2:28). Nothing builds your faith and makes you feel better about the future than reading what God says about it. The Bible says, "Hope deferred makes the heart sick, but when the desire comes, it is a tree of life" (Proverbs 13:12). If your adult child has become heartsick because her (his) desire for the future has been a long time in coming and answered prayer has been delayed, ask God to fill her (his) heart with hope in His name, joy in His presence, and comfort in His Word.

Jeremiah said that when you trust God and put your hope in Him, you are like a tree planted by the water and your roots spread by the river and therefore you don't have to fear when the heat is on in your life. You don't have to be anxious in a drought (Jeremiah 17:7–8). If you ever have been in a drought, you know how frightening that can be. When you are out of water, you realize what a precious and vital commodity it is, for you have no life without it. When you or your adult children are in a dry place,

God will pour living water on both you and them, and hope will rise in your hearts.

Remember That God Is Merciful and Compassionate

At one point Jeremiah had lost all hope. Things were so terrible that he didn't even remember what it was like to feel hopeful anymore. But then he remembered *God's mercy.* "This I recall to my mind, therefore I have hope. Through the LORD'S mercies we are not consumed, because His compassions fail not. They are new every morning; great is Your faithfulness. 'The LORD is my portion,' says my soul, 'Therefore I hope in Him!' " (Lamentations 3:21–24).

No matter what has happened in the past — even as recently as last night — God's mercy is new today. Sin can be repented of today. God can do the impossible today. Things can change today. Hope can fill your heart today.

Jeremiah talked about the necessity of *waiting on the Lord.* That means being patient to wait for God to answer your prayers. "The LORD is good to those who wait for Him, to the soul who seeks Him. It is good that one should hope and wait quietly for the salvation of the LORD" (Lamentations 3:25–26). Waiting on the Lord is hopeful anticipation of what God is going to do. It's trusting that what He is going to do is worth the wait.

Jeremiah also remembered that *God will always show compassion.* We don't suffer forever. "The Lord will not cast off forever. Though He causes grief, yet He will show compassion according to the multitude of His mercies. For He does not afflict willingly, nor grieve the children of men" (Lamentations 3:31–33). It is not His will that we suffer, but He allows suffering to teach us His ways. Remembering that God is merciful and compassionate helps you to keep praying, knowing that He will soon show His mercy and compassion to you and your adult children.

Remember to Send a Letter to Your Son or Daughter About Their Future

If you or I were to be taken to heaven today, there would probably be some things we wish we would have told our adult children. I've written a letter you can write out in your own words, or just write out this one in your own handwriting, and either give it to your adult children now or put it in a place where they will read it later. Ask God to show you the right time for them to receive it. I hope this letter will inspire you to say much more than I have said here.

Dear ______________________________,

I am writing you this letter because I want to tell you that I love you and I am proud of you. I see all the greatness, the gifts, and the talents God has put in you, and I know He is going to use them to do great things through you. I may not have been the perfect parent, and you may not have been the perfect child, but God knew we were perfect for each other. And we all know now that no one is perfect except the Lord. I thank Him every day for you and the wonderful blessing you are, and have always been, to my life.

I have been praying for you — and will continue to pray for you as long as I am alive — that you will have a long and wonderful future. God says that if you believe in Him and trust Him, you can't even imagine how great the future is that He has for you. But it doesn't happen without prayer. We have to pray and pray and keep on praying.

I pray that your relationship with God will be close and strong, and that you will grow in love for His Word and His ways. I pray He will pour out His Spirit afresh on you every day, for He has given you His Holy Spirit to guide you, teach you, comfort you, heal you, set you free, increase your faith, and speak to your heart. I pray that you will always sense His presence and never shut Him out of your life.

Remember that life lived with God is not without challenges, because you will always have an enemy trying to bring you down. May God give you strength to meet those challenges and wisdom to stand strong against the opposition. Always keep in mind that just as God has a plan for your future, so does the enemy. And the enemy will always challenge God's plan for your life. I pray that God's plan will succeed and the enemy's will fail.

As long as you walk close to the Lord, live in obedience to His ways, continue reading His Word, refuse to doubt Him, exalt Him with praise and worship, allow His love to motivate you in all your relationships, seek Him for every decision you make, commit each day to Him, and pray to God in Jesus' name about everything, you cannot go wrong. Ask God to help you do all that.

No matter what happens, do not give up

on the Lord, for He will never give up on you. God never changes. He is the same yesterday, today, and forever (Hebrews 13:8). He has promised many things to you, including hope and a great future. So no matter what happens to you or in your life, those promises will always stand.

Every day put your future in God's hands, because the most important thing about your future is what *He* says and does about it. *He* is your future. Your future will be found by walking with Him today. When you do that, God will be preparing you each day for the future He has for you. Don't get discouraged if things don't seem to be happening as quickly as you would like. They seldom do. That's because while God is making things happen in your life, He is also doing an even more important work inside of you. There are lessons He wants you to learn. Ask Him to help you learn them well.

I may be around for a long time or I may be gone tomorrow. Whatever happens, I have prayed about every aspect of your life. When I die, I will be in heaven with the Lord, but my love and prayers for you will be with you always. I want to be sure that one day I will see you in heaven too. I want you to be able to say, "I have fought the good fight, I have finished the race, I have kept the faith. Finally, there is laid up for me the crown of righteousness, which the Lord, the righteous Judge, will give to me on that Day, and not to me only but also to all who have loved His appearing" (2 Timothy 4:7–8). God says that when you receive Jesus into your heart, your eternal future in heaven is secure. Make sure your future stays secure by never turning your back on the Lord.

Finally, I say to you these words of hope from the Lord, "Arise, shine; for your light has come! And the glory of the LORD is risen upon you. For behold, the darkness shall cover the earth, and deep darkness the people; but the LORD will arise over you, and His glory will be seen upon you" (Isaiah 60:1–2). Remember that even in the dark times of your life, the light of Jesus *in* you and *upon* you can never be put out.

I love you always,

____

Lord, I pray for (name of adult child) to have a future that is good, long, prosperous, and secure because it is in Your hands. Thank You that Your thoughts toward her (him) are thoughts of peace and to give her (him) a future and a hope (Jeremiah 29:11). Guide her (him) step by step so that she (he) never gets off the path You have for her (his) life. Turn her (his) heart toward You so that she (he) always has Your will and Your ways in mind. Keep her (him) from wasting time on a pathway that You will not bless.

Help her (him) to run the race in the right way, so she (he) will finish strong and receive the prize You have for her (him) (1 Corinthians 9:24). I pray that she (he) will be planted firmly in Your house so that she (he) will flourish in Your courts and will always be fresh and flourishing and bear fruit into old age (Psalm 92:13–15). Help her (him) to remember that You are "able to do exceedingly abundantly above all that we ask or think, according to the power that works in us" (Ephesians 3:20).

I pray that nothing will ever separate her (him) from Your love, which is found in Christ Jesus (Romans 8:38–39). Thank You, Holy Spirit, that You will always be with her (him) to guide her (him) and teach her (him), and bring comfort in difficult times. I pray that her (his) future will continue to grow brighter with every passing day. I pray that her (his) ultimate future is in heaven with You, and that I will be there to see her (him) again.

I pray that You — the God of hope — will fill her (him) with Your joy and peace so that she (he) will "abound in hope by the power of the Holy Spirit" (Romans 15:13).

In Jesus' name I pray.

Blessed is the man who trusts in the LORD, and whose hope is the LORD. For he shall be like a tree planted by the waters, which spreads out its roots by the river, and will not fear when heat comes; but its leaf will be green, and will not be anxious in the year of drought, nor will cease from yielding fruit.

JEREMIAH 17:7–8

Mark the blameless man, and observe the upright; for the future of that man is peace.

PSALM 37:37

But the path of the just is like the shining sun, that shines ever brighter unto the perfect day.

PROVERBS 4:18

There is surely a future hope for you, and your hope will not be cut off.

PROVERBS 23:18 NIV

Eye has not seen, nor ear heard, nor have entered into the heart of man the things which God has prepared for

those who love Him.
1 CORINTHIANS 2:9

ABOUT THE AUTHOR

Stormie Omartian is the bestselling author of The Power of a Praying® series (more than 13 million copies sold worldwide), which includes *The Power of a Praying® Wife* and *The Power of a Praying® Husband.* Her many other books include *Just Enough Light for the Step I'm On, The Prayer That Changes Everything®, The Power of a Praying® Woman, The Power of Praying® Through the Bible,* and *The Power of Prayer to Change Your Marriage.* Stormie and her husband, Michael, have been married more than 35 years and are the parents of two adult children.